BCBA

Exam Study Prep
Crash Course

Handbook Of Applied Behavior Analysis
to Master the
5th Edition Task List.

Linda Cooper

Table of Contents

Section 1: Foundations

A   **Philosophical Underpinnings**

B   **Concepts and Principles**

C   **Measurement, Data Display, and Interpretation**

D   **Experimental Design**

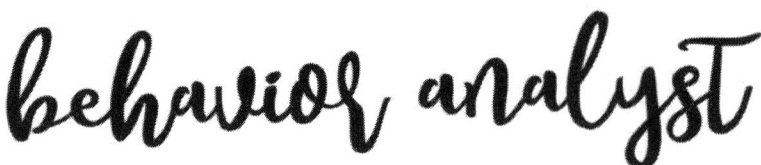

behavior analyst

(n.): a smile bringing, environment manipulating, data collecting rockstar who lives to understand behavior and loves to improve the lives of others by applying evidence-based interventions.

See also: behavior whisperer

A.   **Philosophical Underpinnings**

A-1: Identify the goals of behaviour analysis as a science (i.e., description, prediction, control)

A-2: Explain the philosophical assumptions underlying the science of behaviour analysis (e.g., selectionism, determinism, empiricism, parsimony, pragmatism)

A-3: Describe and explain behaviour from the perspective of radical behaviourism

A-4: Distinguish among behaviourism, the experimental analysis of behaviour, applied behaviour analysis, and professional practice guided by the science of behaviour analysis

A-5: Describe and define the dimensions of applied behaviour analysis (Baer, Wolf, & Risley, 1968)

A-1 Identify The Goals Of Behavior Analysis As A Science

Science
A systematic approach for seeking and organizing knowledge about the world. It aims to discover nature's truth about phenomena.

Description
Systematic observation of events that can be quantified, classified, and examined for possible relations with other known facts. It enhances understanding of a given phenomenon by enabling scientists to describe it accurately and often suggests possible hypotheses or questions for additional research. ("I know what the behavior looks/ sounds like.")
Observe + describe with objective statements.
E.g., A friend calls you up and asks how your day was. You begin to describe to your friend that you had a terrible day; you woke up late, spilled your coffee all over your shirt, and were late to work. You have provided your friend a quantifiable description of your terrible morning.

Prediction (AKA: Correlation, Covariation)
Repeated observations reveal that two events consistently co-vary with each other; this correlation can be used to predict the relative probability that one event will occur based on the presence of another event ("I know when the behavior will occur.").
It cannot demonstrate functional relations since no variables are manipulated but can suggest the possibility of exploring causal relations.
Prediction enables preparation.
E.g., You observe your neighbor collect the mail in their driveway every afternoon. You also observe that your neighbor carries an umbrella over their head when it's raining. You can predict that your neighbor will have an umbrella each time it rains while they collect their mail.
E.g. During the winter, people get more colds. It's a prediction but not a guarantee or a cause. I can get a cold also during spring or summer.

Control (AKA: Causation)
The ability to predict with a certain degree of confidence is the highest level of understanding. A functional relationship exists when the manipulation of an independent variable can produce a reliable change in a dependent variable that is unlikely the result of extraneous (confounding) variables. ("I can turn this behavior on and off like a faucet.")
E.g., A client in a residential treatment facility engages in self-injurious behavior, and has been referred for a functional analysis. During the analysis, the client does not engage in self-injury during the play (control), attention, or tangible conditions. During the demand condition, however, the client engages in self-injury whenever they are presented with a demand. Removing the demand consistently results in the termination of the self-injurious behavior.

A-2 Explain The Philosophical Assumptions Underlying The Science Of Behavior Analysis

These attitudes of science constitute a set of overriding assumptions and values that guide the work of all scientists.

Selectionism

It describes the process of change over time in the organism's biological status (natural selection), its behavior, and its behavior in relation to other organisms (culture) due to interactions with its environment. Evolution is the product of a functional selection.

B. F. Skinner said there are 3 ways the environment can apply itself to a living being: Phylogenic, Ontogenic, and Cultural.

1.   Phylogenic: Selection in the evolutionary history of a species (aka Darwinism).

It can be a natural process of genetic survival characteristics passed on to future generations. (E.g.,a giraffe with a longer neck for better survival chance). It can also be guided via artificial selective manipulation (E.g.,selective animal breeding).

2.   Ontogenic: This refers to the selection of behavior by consequences over an individual's lifetime. How the environment changes an individual behavior over time? There are natural consequences and planned contingencies.

3.   Cultural: Passing behavior from one person to another by imitation and modeling. This includes common rules and contingencies of behavior involving others.

Determinism

It's the scientific assumption that the universe is a lawful and orderly place where all phenomena occur systematically as the result of other events. Nothing is random; events do not happen "out of the blue." Events have causes and effects, and we can learn them.

(NOT indeterminism – events are not predictable nor controllable because of "free will"; NOT fatalism - events are predetermined by destiny; NOT predestination – God controls all events)

E.g., An RBT working with a client observes them engaging in self-injurious behavior seemingly "out of nowhere." The RBT decides to seek further support from a supervisor, as they do not accept the possibility that self-injury could arise for no reason. The supervisor then designs an assessment process to help determine what might be contributing to the self-injury.

Empiricism

Objective observation of the phenomena of interest, independent of subject opinions or personal beliefs. The scientist objectively observes, measures events, and collects data on the phenomenon of interest.

Knowledge comes from experimentation and experience.

Remember: Empiricism-evidence-data-facts

Experimentation (AKA: Experimental Analysis)

An experiment is a carefully conducted comparison of a dependent variable under 2 or more different conditions in which only the independent variable varies from one condition to another. This is used to investigate the possible existence of a functional relation.

E.g., During therapy sessions, your client perseverates on when their parents are coming to visit. This behavior has become very difficult to redirect using simple verbal statements. You introduce the use of a visual calendar to show your client what day of the week their parent comes to visit. Before you begin your therapy sessions, you start by reviewing the visual calendar with your client. The client does not ask when their parents are coming to visit for the entirety of your session. Then, you remove the visual calendar, and the target behavior returns. You then reintroduce it, and the target behavior goes down once more. The introduction of the visual schedule (independent variable) appeared to affect the amount of time the client spends perseverating on their parent visits (dependent variable).

Replication

Repeating experiments to determine the reliability of effects and increase internal validity.
Also used to assess the generality of findings to other subjects, settings, and behaviors.
It is needed for a finding to be accepted as a pattern or eventually to discover mistakes in the repeated process.

Parsimony

Before more complex or abstract explanations are considered, all simple, logical explanations for phenomena must be ruled out.
Choose the explanation for a phenomenon that requires the fewest assumptions; it is usually the correct one.
E.g., A client at a group home was recently up all night, disturbing other residents. Staff assumed that the overnight worker forgot to give the client their nighttime medication. The staff nurse at the group home reviewed the consumer's medication administration record and saw that he didn't receive their nighttime medication on time, so this is the explanation for his disrupted sleep.

Philosophical Doubt

The truthfulness and validity of science should be continually questioned. A good scientist maintains a healthy level of skepticism and is always open to new data leading to new interpretations or explanations of the phenomenon. Question the truth and be open to be wrong.

"Change and be ready to change again. Accept no eternal verity. Experiment." (Skinner, 1979)

E.g., A newly hired behavior analyst reviews a patient's records dating back three years from the current date. The functional analysis results indicate that aggression toward others served a function of attention. However, interventions have not been successful at reducing aggression. Rather than relying on three years old records, the new behavior analyst conducts a further assessment to determine if the original assessment still holds true. This new behavior analyst is operating under philosophical doubt since they are demonstrating a healthy amount of skepticism about the results of a previously conducted functional analysis.

Pragmatism

The truth or value of a scientific statement is determined by how it promotes effective action.
A theory is true if it's useful, our science needs to improve the lives of others. This introduces the relative, individual truth and invites customizing solutions to individual needs instead of "one treatment fits all." Offers a conceptual framework for "best practice" regarding client needs. A probabilistic AB-because of C-philosophy. An idea lies in its observable practical consequences, rather than in theory.
Acronym: DEERPP

Mentalism (AKA: Spiritual, Psychic, Feelings, Attitudes, Subjective, Processing)

To understand what makes our science behavioral we have to understand mentalism.
It explains behavior through assumptions about the existence of an inner and mental dimen-

tion as the cause of behavior.
It includes:

- Hypothetical constructs: Presumed but unobserved process. Free will, self-esteem, readiness, etc. as causes of behavior that can't be observed or manipulated.
E.g., He passed the test because he is intelligent
- Explanatory Fictions: Attributing an unobservable process to behavior. E.g., knowing, wanting, figuring out, understanding.
- Cicular Reasoning: The cause and effect are both inferred from the same info. What came first? The chicken or the egg?
E.g., Sam cried because he felt sad.
E.g., Sam cursed because he has bad manners.

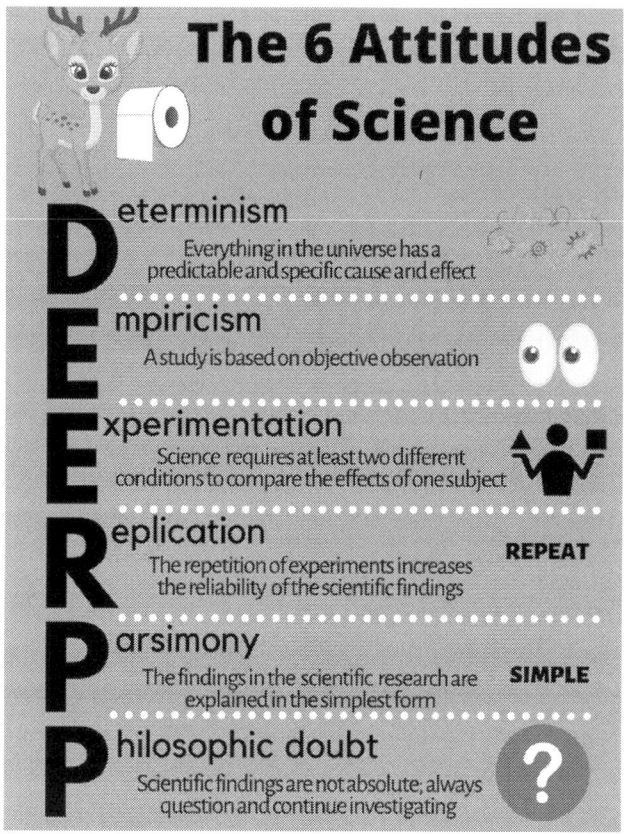

A-3 Describe And Explain Behavior From The Perspective Of Radical Behaviorism

Some History

1850-early 1900s: Ivan Pavlov and Classical Conditioning (AKA Pavlovian Conditioning, S-S Pairing, Conditioned Stimulus-Conditioned Response). Respondent conditioning with dogs.

1913 John Watson and Methodological Behaviorism (AKA Stimulus-Response Behaviorism, S-R Psychology, Watsonian Behaviorism). Only looks at publicly observable events in the analysis of behavior and it excludes private events.

1938-1990s B.F. Skinner and Radical Behaviorism

Radical Behaviorism

Radical behaviorism is the philosophy of the science of behavior (analysis). It's the school of thought pioneered by B. F. Skinner that argues that behavior, rather than mental states, should be the focus of study in psychology. Skinner uses the term "radical" to relate behaviorism to its origins (behavior). It rejects mentalism and focuses on objective and measurable behavior. It attempts to explain all behavior, including private events, thoughts and feelings, and verbal behavior.

Private events are distinguished from other "public" behavior only by their inaccessibility, but the same variables influence them. Individuals can be taught to name their private events and communicate their emotions and feelings.

Radical behaviorism is the basic foundation of all the domains of behavior analysis.

E.g., Your client engages in intense ritual behaviors, including wearing certain clothing items at certain times of the day. When you try to interrupt the client's engagement in the ritual, they become extremely aggressive toward you. A team member suggests that feelings of frustration cause this behavior. As a radical behaviorist, you do not operate under the assumption that emotions cause behaviors. Instead, feelings can make things in the environment more or less valuable.

A-4 Distinguish Among Behaviorism, The Experimental Analysis Of Behavior, Applied Behavior Analysis, And Professional Practice Guided By The Science Of Behavior Analysis

Behaviorism (AKA: Conceptual Analysis of Behavior)

Philosophy of the science of behavior, started by Watson as a rection to Mentalism, informs all other domains of behavior analysis. It addresses philosophical, theoretical, historical, and methodological issues in the field of the science of behavior analysis.

It emphasizes objective methods of investigation and is rooted in the assumption that behavior results from interactions between the environment and individual variables (such as prior learning history). Environmental (not mentalistic) explanation of behavior.

Radical Behaviorism (see A-3)

It's the first branch and focuses on the philosophy and theory of our science and where we started.

Experimental Analysis of Behavior (EAB)

This is basic research. EAB work is conducted under controlled conditions, primarily in laboratory settings. It consists of single-subject experiments with human and nonhuman subjects to discover, extend, and clarify fundamental principles of behavior.

Four methodologies characterize this unique approach:
- Direct, repeated measurement of behavior
- Rate of response as the basic datum (#of responses/time)
- Graphed data
- Within-subject comparisons

E.g., Researchers study the effects of multiple schedules of reinforcement on skill acquisition in rats.

Applied Behavior Analysis (ABA)

This is applied research, the actual practice, and the application of basic ABA principles derived from EAB to solve problems of social significance. It uses systematic manipulations to determine the functional relation between behavior and the environment in a natural setting. It's the applied experiment to improve behavior: increase/decrease existing behavior, teach a new behavior, teach in which specific conditions emit a behavior.

Creates behavior-change tactics and the technology for improving behavior.

E.g., A practitioner uses the science of behavior to bring about socially meaningful outcomes for clients.

Professional Practice guided by the Science Of Behavior Analysis

It's the delivery of ABA interventions by other people or professionals to consumers. Everyone can learn and use behavior change tactics: teachers, parents, RBT, sport coaches, etc.

Also think that ABA can be used in job safety, health, business, animal training, commerce, sports, etc.

One primary function includes training and implementing behavioral technologies for direct staff and support.

E.g., A health care provider coaches a caregiver on praising a patient's cooperative behavior.

DOMAINS OF BEHAVIOR ANALYSIS

Applied Behavior Analysis

- Applied research
- ABA applies principles/theories to solve socially significant problems
- Natural environment
- Generally focuses on humans
- Aligns with 7 Dimensions of ABA
- Develops technologies for practitioners

Behavior Service Delivery

- Professional practice to solve problems for clients
- Use of technologies to address immediate needs of the client
- Natural environment
- Socially valid methods/results
- Results focus on current bx or setting & remediating symptoms

Philosophy and Conceptual Analysis

- Informs the other domains of behavior analysis
- Radical Behaviorism is the underlying philosophy
- All behavior (private & public) follows the same principles

Experimental Analysis of Behavior

- Theory driven research that focuses on processes
- Conducted across species in lab/contrived settings
- Quality results demonstrate experimental control
- Discovers principles and theories

A-5 Describe And Define The Dimensions Of Applied Behavior Analysis (Baer, Wolf, & Risley, 1968)

Applied
Select behaviors to change that are socially significant (social, language, academic, daily living, self-care, vocational, and/or recreation and leisure) to enhance and improve people's life. The outcome must be meaningful for the person.

Behavioral
Observable and measurable behaviors are targeted. The behavior description needs to be clear, concise, complete, objective, and operational.
(Be careful! Sometimes behavior can be behavioral but not applied)

Analytic (AKA: Functional Relation, Experimentation, Control, Causation)
A functional relation is demonstrated by systematically manipulating environmental events.

Technological
A written description of all procedures in the study is clear, complete, and detailed to enable others to replicate it.

Conceptually Systematic
Procedures and behavior change interventions are derived from basic principles of behavior. (i.e., reinforcement, extinction, punishment, etc.)

Effective
Interventions are monitored to evaluate the impact on the target behavior.
Data shows that the behavior improved sufficiently to produce practical results for the participant(s). It answers the question: does the procedure work?

Generality (AKA Generalization)
Behavior changes should maintain and transfer across subjects, appear in other environments, or spread to other behaviors.

Acronym: "GET A CAB"!
Easy right?

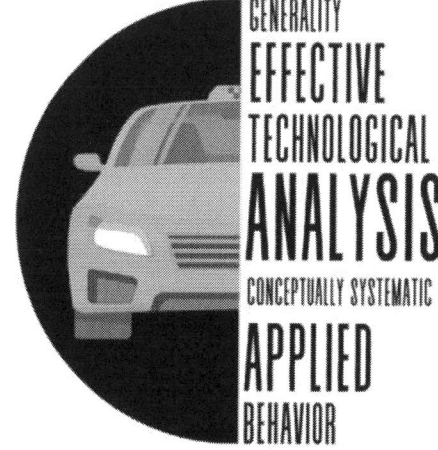

Coffee and Notes:

B. Concepts and Principles

B-1: Define and provide examples of behaviour, response, and response class

B-2: Define and provide examples of stimulus and stimulus class

B-3: Define and provide examples of respondent and operant conditioning

B-4: Define and provide examples of positive and negative reinforcement contingencies

B-5: Define and provide examples of schedules of reinforcement

B-6: Define and provide examples of positive and negative punishment contingencies

B-7: Define and provide examples of automatic and socially mediated contingencies

B-8: Define and provide examples of unconditioned, conditioned, and generalized reinforcers and punishers

B-9: Define and provide examples of operant extinction.

B-10: Define and provide examples of stimulus control

B-11: Define and provide examples of discrimination, generalization, and maintenance

B-12: Define and provide examples of motivating operations

B-13: Define and provide examples of rule-governed and contingency-shaped behaviour

B-14: Define and provide examples of the verbal operants

B-15: Define and provide examples of derived stimulus relations

B-1 Define And Provide Examples Of Behavior, Response, And Response Class

Response

A single instance (one occurrence) of behavior.

E.g., jumping is the behavior; every single jump is one response.

Behavior

Collective term for multiple instances of a response.

Any activity or interaction with the environment of a living organism (NO objects, NO organizations). Behaver is the individual who is behaving.

Behavior involves active action and anything a dead man can't do (the "Dead Man" test).

Attention! It could be inside the organism (private behavior), but the behavior is not a state of being.

Examples: ring a bell, touch your head, eat, breathe, think, imagine, feel pain, etc.

Non-examples:

- The car speeds; Italy recovers losses; The computer shuts down. (NO living organisms)
- I received a letter; The bus was taking me to school; The kid didn't comply. (NO action, a Dead Man CAN do it)
- I am tired; He was anxious; She is intelligent, I know/understand (State of being or Traits, Mentalistic terminology)

Tip: If you can't operationally define it, it's not behavior.

Response Class

A group of topographically different responses (they can look different) that have the same effect in the environment (they serve the same function).

E.g., Saying "water," pointing to the water bottle, and getting the water from the fridge are all topographically different responses with the same function of getting the water.

E.g., A patient engages in head banging, screaming, and hitting staff which all produce the same effect on the environment (such as escape from activities).

The response class is the Dependent Variable (DV), studied to see the effect of the independent variable (IV).

Repertoire

A collection of skills that an individual has learned related to a specific task or setting.

E.g., speaking different languages, cooking, self-care routines, etc.

B-2 Define And Provide Examples Of Stimulus And Stimulus Class

Environment

It's the full set of physical circumstances in which the organism exists: anything and everything surrounding a learner. Behavior can't occur without an environment.

E.g., furniture, other people, the beach, etc.

Stimulus

A change in the environment that a person can experience through their senses and affects their behavior. It's anything that can be seen, heard, smelled, felt, or tasted. A stimulus is characterized by its onset/offset, magnification/attenuation, something added/removed.

E.g., louder music, vibration from a phone, light turning on/off (note that a constant light is not a stimulus because there's no change)

E.g., The presence of your boss during a usually boss-free weekly collaboration meeting.

3 human body systems are impacted by stimuli:
- Proprioceptors: receive stimulation from joints and muscles needed for posture, balance, and movement.
- Interoceptors: receive stimulation from organs. E.g., headache, hunger pains.
- Exteroceptors: the 5 senses (hearing, seeing, touching, smiling, and tasting). Most often studied by behavior analysts.

E.g., smelling smoke, tasting a meal, hearing noises, etc.

Acronym: PIE

Stimulus Class

A group of stimuli that share one or more common formal, temporal or functional characteristics, and that tend to evoke or abate the same behavior or response class.

3 types of stimulus classes:
- Formal: physical features, shapes, sizes, color, weight, spatial positions in relation to other objects (what it looks like)
- Temporal: refers to the same position in time with respect to the behavior. An antecedent refers to environmental conditions that occur prior to the behavior of interest; a consequence is a stimulus change that follows the behavior of interest. Antecedent and consequent stimuli determine what's learned.
- Functional: refers to the effect of the stimulus on the behavior, the function (evoke/abate, strengthen/weaken behavior).

Note: stimuli can only share the functional characteristic if they also share the temporal one.

Only antecedents evoke/abate behavior in the present; only consequences strengthen/weaken behavior in the future.

E.g., bright sunlight, turning a light on in the middle of the night, and strong winds, all cause a person to squint their eyes. (same function)

The stimulus class is the Independent Variable (IV); it's the one we manipulate.

Acronym: FTF (For The Fun)

Another way to classify Stimulus classes is by:

- Feature stimulus class: similar to the Formal type, collects stimuli that share the same topographies. It is created by stimulus generalization.

E.g., the concept of dog, the concept of chair, etc.

- Arbitrary stimulus class: collects stimuli that evoke the same response but that don't look alike. It is created by stimulus equivalence.

E.g., an apple and a banana don't look alike but are members of the class of fruits.

E.g., Saying I want 50%, half, or ½ of your profits evokes the same response.

B-3 Define And Provide Examples Of Respondent And Operant Conditioning

There are 2 primary types of behavior: Respondent behavior and Operant behavior.

1.   Respondent Behavior (AKA: Reflex, Reflexive Relations, US-UR)

Involuntary behavior that is elicited without any prior learning. It is part of an organism's genetic endowment (Phylogenic) and is elicited by antecedents. No history of consequences! It's a product of natural evolution because it can protect our species.

E.g, US (Unconditioned Stimulus): Doctor strikes your knee

UR (Unconditioned Response): Leg going up

Habituation

When the unconditioned stimulus is presented repeatedly over a short period of time the strength of the respondent behavior diminishes.

E.g., I smell something bad, at first I gag then my response weakens and I gag less frequently.

Respondent Conditioning (AKA: Pavlovian Conditioning, Classic Conditioning, S-S pairing, CS-CR)

Introduced by Ivan Pavlov (does that name ring a bell?), it's the process of pairing a neutral stimulus with either an unconditioned or conditioned stimulus that results in a new reflex relation.

The stimulus elicits a response (S-R contingency).

The topography and basic functions are predetermined: eye blink, lacrimal secretion (tears), sneezing, coughing, shivering, sweating, vomiting, salivating, hand/foot withdrawal, and activation syndrome.

The process is the following:

•   Before conditioning: Reflex. Respondent behavior is elicited by antecedent stimuli (S-R relation). An unconditioned stimulus (US) elicits an involuntary response (UR). No prior learning is required.

US -->UR (Food elicits salivation, no consequence)

NS --> No response (A bell doesn't evoke any response)

•   During conditioning: Neutral stimuli (NS) can acquire the ability to elicit respondents through the learning process of respondent conditioning.

NS + US --> UR (The bell and the food are paired multiple times)

•   After conditioning: The NS is now a conditioned stimulus (CS) that elicits a conditioned response. (CR)

CS --> CR (The bell elicits salivation, still without consequence!)

Note that CR is the same behavior as UR.

E.g., Jane salivates when Danny describes the sushi he just ate for dinner. (Conditioned Reflex)

E.g., The fire alarm at work was previously a neutral stimulus. Then, you had a fire drill while you were standing right next to the alarm! The sound hurt your ears and was quite unpleasant. Through respondent conditioning (pairing of the neutral fire alarm with the aversive sound), you now cringe each time you see the fire alarm, even when it is not going off.

Conditioning=Pairing (NOT learning!)

Why was Pavlov's hair so soft? Because he conditioned it!

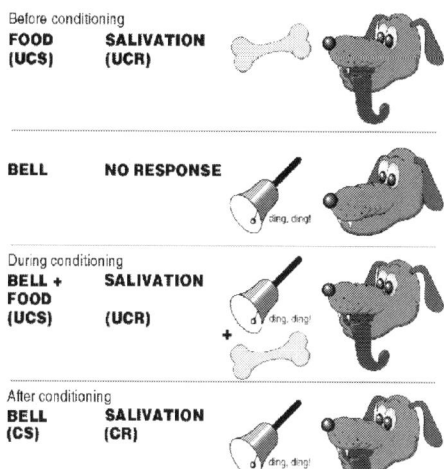

Respondent Extinction

The conditioned reflex would eventually weaken if a conditioned stimulus is presented without the unconditioned stimulus for a given period of time. The bell doesn't elicit salivation if it's not paired with the meat for a long time. The bell eventually loses its eliciting power and goes back to its neutral status (NS).

2.   Operant Behavior (AKA: ABC, 3 Term Contingency, S-R-S Model)

An operant behavior is a behavior determined and maintained by a history of consequences. It's a voluntary and learned behavior, and it's the result of interaction with the environment and the following consequences (Ontogenic). It's the result of the A-B-C relation.

It is defined by function, not by topography.

It's evoked/emitted (vs elicited for respondent behavior).

E.g., writing, reading, dancing, remembering a poem, cooking, etc.

Adaptation

With a repeated presentation of a particular stimulus, response reduces. It is the operant version of habituation that occurs for respondent behaviors.

E.g., after you hear the same joke multiple times, you laugh less.

Operant Conditioning (AKA: ABC, 3 Term Contingency, Behavioral Contingency)

B.F. Skinner coined the term Operant Conditioning and studied it by conducting experiments using animals, mainly rats, placing them in what he called the "Skinner Box." It's the process of learning through consequences, reinforcement, and punishment. R-S or S-R-S contingency.

A stimulus change following a response closely in time increases (reinforcement) or decreases (punishment) future occurrences of similar responses under similar conditions. So, behaviors are strengthened or weakened. The selection of behavior by consequences operates during the individual organism's lifetime (ontogeny) and by natural selection (phylogeny).

Consequences can only affect future behavior.

Immediate consequences have the greatest effect.

Operant conditioning occurs automatically, regardless of whether the individual is aware that they are being reinforced. (Automaticity of reinforcement and punishment)

E.g., I see a pizza, and I take a bite. (Operant) - I see a pizza, and I salivate. (Respondent)

I pedal my bike from home to school (Operant) – I pedal, and my body sweat (Respondent)

E.g., Your cell phone lights up, and you see a text from an acquaintance. You respond to the text message. The conversation continues through text, and you enjoy the interaction. You are likely to answer the next time the person texts you. (Operant)

Respondent and operant conditioning can occur simultaneously.

Consequences
A stimulus change that comes after the behavior and affects future behavior.

3 Principles of Behavior
• Reinforcement
• Punishment
• Extinction

Every ABA strategy is derived from those 3 principles (Conceptually Systematic).

B-4 Define And Provide Examples Of Positive And Negative Reinforcement Contingencies
(View Task List G-1)

Reinforcement

An environmental change follows a response closely in time, is contingent on that response, and increases the probability of similar responses under similar circumstances.

It changes what comes before the behavior (antecedents) and what comes after the behavior (consequences). It creates stimulus control, making responding in the presence of the SD more likely. Discriminated Operant is a behavior that occurs in some conditions (SD) more than in others.

Reinforcement doesn't only strengthen rate, it can also strengthen duration, latency, magnitude, and topography. The immediacy of the reinforcer is critical (Temporal relation).

Note that only behavior can be reinforced, not people.

Positive Reinforcement (AKA: SR+, Type 1 Reinforcement)

It occurs when a response is followed immediately by the presentation of a desirable or pleasant stimulus that increases the future occurrence of similar responses. To strengthen a behavior means making it occur more often, but it could also mean altering its duration, latency, IRT, magnitude, and/or topography.

E.g., After a child does her chores, she receives a cookie. The cookie increases the likelihood that the child will do her tasks again in the future.

Types of Positive reinforcement could include:
- Social consequences: praise, rewards, hugs, high five
- Tangible items, toys, or activities
- Edibles
- Sensory toys or activities

Praises are the easiest reinforcers to deliver, at no cost, natural and quick. We should always try to start reinforcing with praises or pair them with other types of reinforcers.

E.g., of Praise: if a teacher praises the students for doing a great job working in groups, the students will likely collaborate well in groups again in the future.

E.g., of Rewards: Sometimes, places of work will offer rewards for various work-related tasks. They may offer a reward for the employee with the most sales in a month. The employee is likely to continue to make more sales in the future.

Some general guidelines for increasing the effectiveness of positive reinforcement are:
- Set an easily achievable initial criterion for reinforcement: we want the child to be able to earn the reinforcement easily, then increase the criterion slowly over time
- Initially reinforce every occurrence of behavior (FR1), then gradually shift to a less dense schedule of reinforcement, intermittent and delayed schedules.
- Use high-quality reinforcers of sufficient magnitude.
- Vary the reinforcers: repeated exposure to the same item may increase the risk of satiation.
- Use direct reinforcement contingencies when possible: completing the task itself produces the reinforcement without the practitioner's intervention.
- Combine response prompts and reinforcement
- Provide contingent attention and descriptive praise
- Gradually increase the response-reinforcement delay

- Shift progressively from contrived to naturally occurring reinforcers
- Minimize the use of potentially dangerous reinforcers that may harm the client's health and development. (candies, sugar, chips, cigarettes, etc....)

Negative Reinforcement (AKA: SR-, Type 2 Reinforcement, Reinforcement by Relief)

The removal of an aversive stimulus following a response increases the likelihood of the targeted behavior in the future. It's also called Reinforcement by Relief because an irritant or something aversive is removed.

E.g., Jane has a bad headache, so she takes medicine, and the pain goes away. Jane will take medication every time she has a headache. (the pain is removed)

E.g., You wake up in the morning with a terrible cramp in your neck. You turn your neck right and left to crack it, which causes the pain to go away. Each time you wake up with a cramp in your neck, you will engage in the response (cracking your neck) to remove the pain.

Two types of Negative Reinforcement:
- Escape: a behavior that stops an ongoing aversive stimulus or unpleasant situation. The aversive is already happening. E.g., Turning off the loud music is escaping from loud music.
- Avoidance: more common than escape. A response that prevents or postpones the presentation of an aversive stimulus or unpleasant situation. The aversive never occurs.
- Discriminated avoidance: the behavior to prevent the aversive occurs in the presence of a signal/SD. E.g., I avoid taking the freeway this morning because I saw on the GPS that there is an accident.
- Free operant avoidance: the behavior to prevent the aversive occurs without the presence of an SD. E.g., I avoid taking the freeway during rush hours without looking if there is traffic or not.

Automatic Reinforcement (AKA: Sensory, Self-Stimulatory Behaviors, Stereotypy) View Task List B-7

Reinforcement occurs without a social mediation of others. It can mean naturally produced sensory consequences.

Positive Automatic Reinforcement: E.g., I taste apple pie for the 1st time and now I bake it all the time at home.

Negative Automatic Reinforcement: E.g., Rachel's back is itching, she scratches it, and the itch goes away. She scratches her back more often in the future.

Positive Automatic Punishment: E.g., My Prada sweater itch, in the future I don't buy that sweater brand anymore.

Negative Automatic Punishment: E.g., I bite my nails but the nail polish goes away, in the future, I bite my nails less frequently.

Important Note:

Positive (+): something is added to the environment, presented

Negative (-): something is removed from the environment, terminated

Reinforcement: increase the future occurrence of that response in the future (>)

Punishment: decrease the future occurrence of that response in the future (<)

Unwanted Effects Of Reinforcement

- Satiation of the reinforcer
- Avoid reinforcers that are harmful to the health and development of the client or that may require excessive Mos to be effective.
- Delivery of the reinforcer can be distracting.

•   Behavioral Contrast: This describes the effects of a schedule change that increases or decreases the rate of responding in one schedule of reinforcement and results in an opposite change of responding in the other schedule of reinforcement where no intervention has been put into place. To avoid the contrast effect, always program the procedure in all settings in which the behavior occurs.

- Positive Behavioral Contrast occurs when the behavior increases in the non-treatment setting and decreases in the treatment condition. E.g., Lina stops talking to me (my behavior is put on extinction), so I talk more with Sofia even if she didn't do anything different (my behavior increased even if nothing changed here).

- Negative Behavioral Contrast occurs when the behavior decreases in the non-treatment setting and increases in the treatment condition.

•   Transient Effects: when a reinforcer is removed, a change in responding should be expected.

•   A decrease in other functionally equivalent behaviors that are not receiving reinforcement.

•   "Unnatural" contingencies: providing consequences that are not available in the natural environment. This makes it difficult to transition away from the reinforcement (E.g., tokens). The best solution is to program for natural reinforcement contingencies.

•   Undesirable response pattern: schedule of reinforcement used might influence undesirable rates of responding.

•   Narrowing effect on behavior: only a specific response is followed by a reinforcer, this may result in a small number of responses as members of a response class. E.g., "Tell me a vehicle," and John always says "train." A solution is using a lag schedule to promote variation.

•   Shadowing the SD: only attend to the SD established during training and not to the natural antecedent that should control the behavior in the environment. E.g., Jane only responds to the instructions delivered by the BT and not by her mom. A solution is to always program natural antecedents and transfer discriminative control.

•   Strengthening undesired behavior: pay attention to the type of response occurring when the reinforcer is delivered. E.g., Jane completes a task, hits a table, and gets a favorite toy. You need to provide the toy immediately after she completes the task and before she hits the table.

B-5 Define And Provide Examples Of Schedules Of Reinforcement

A schedule of reinforcement is a rule that specifies which responses will be followed by reinforcement, and which will not.

Continuous Reinforcement (CRF or FR1)

The desired behavior is reinforced every single time it occurs. This schedule is best used during the initial stages of learning to create a strong association between the behavior and response.
E.g., Every time I turn the key, the door opens.

Extinction Schedule (EXT)

The behavior is never reinforced. It is used to eliminate the behavior.

Intermittent Schedules Of Reinforcement

Only selected occurrences of behavior produce reinforcement. It is used to maintain behavior and transition from artificial to natural reinforcement. There are 2 types:

1)   Ratio Schedule:

schedule under which reinforcement is delivered after a certain number of correct responses.

- Fixed Ratio (FR)- reinforce every set number of correct responses.

FR1 is also called Continuous Reinforcement (CRF). In fixed schedules, there is a post-reinforcement pause that can be observed in the graphs. For the FR schedule, the responding occurs in a stepwise fashion, with longer pauses before responding increases steadily.
E.g., FR 10: delivering a food pellet to a rat after it presses a bar 10 times.
E.g., You get a snack every time you put in your money and hit the button on the vending machine (FR 1/continuous).

- Variable Ratio (VR)- reinforcement delivered after a variable number of correct responses.

In the graph, we can observe a consistent, steep, and steady rate of responding that doesn't produce a post-reinforcement pause. This schedule is well known for producing higher rates of responding, which is associated with slot machines and gambling.
E.g., VR10: delivering food pellets to a rat after 9 bar presses, after 13 bar presses, and then again after 8 bar presses.
E.g., You study every night. You find something interesting after reading two pages, five pages, two pages, three pages, four pages, and so on. On average, you contact reinforcement (interesting information) after reading three pages (VR 3).

2)   Interval Schedule:

require an elapse of time and one correct response before reinforcement is delivered.
- Fixed Interval (FI)- behavior is reinforced after a set amount of time and 1correct response.
The graph of a FI schedule is a scalloped pattern (hint: FI=FIsh graph) in which we observe a short pause in responding after the delivery of reinforcement then the response gradually increases.
E.g., FI30sec: reinforcing a rat with a lab pellet for the first bar press after a 30-second interval has elapsed.

E.g., You get a paycheck every two weeks for doing your work (FI 2).

• Variable Interval (VI)- reinforcement is delivered after an average amount of time and a correct response. The VI schedule graph shows a steady and consistent responding pattern. The rate of responding is low-to-moderate. It is good for maintenance behaviors.

E.g., VI3min: providing a food pellet to a rat after the first bar press following a 1-minute interval; a second pellet for the first response following a 5minute interval; and a third pellet for the first response following a 3minute interval.

E.g., You are a kid sitting safely in your seat at school. The teacher provides reinforcement for every 10 minutes, 12 minutes,12 minutes, and 13 minutes spent sitting safely. On average, you contact reinforcement every 12 minutes (VI 12).

	Fixed Schedules *Unsteady, Pause-and-burst*	**Variable Schedules** *Steady, Little to no pause*
Ratio schedule Higher rates of responding	**Fixed Ratio FR**	**Variable Ratio VR**
Interval schedule Lower rates of responding	**Fixed Interval FI**	**Variable Interval VI**

Limited Hold (LH)

Restriction on an Interval schedule. Reinforcement remains for a finite time following the elapse of the fixed or variable interval. The participant will miss the opportunity to receive reinforcement if a targeted response does not occur within the time limit.

E.g., The subway passes by every 20min and the door stays open for 1min. After that 1min, the door close, and you need to wait for another interval to get the opportunity to earn the reinforcer of getting on the train. (VI 20min LH1min)

E.g., the student needs to answer 20 questions in the quiz in 30 min (limited hold) to earn reinforcement from the teacher. (FR20 LH30min)

Time-Based Schedule (AKA: Noncontingent reinforcement, NCR)

Stimulus is delivered or removed at a point in time, independent of responding. It can be Fixed time (FT) or Variable Time (VT).

E.g., Jimmy gets a candy every 5 min, regardless of what he's doing. (FT)

Schedule Thinning

Gradually increase the response ratio or time interval prior to delivering the reinforcement.

We normally go from a dense schedule (responses produce a lot of reinforcement) to a thin schedule (responses produce less frequent reinforcement).

E.g., FR2, FR5, FR7...

Ratio Strain

An abrupt increase in the ratio of reinforcement requirements can lead to aggression, avoidance, and unpredictable pauses in responding.

E.g., going from FR2 to FR15, the gap is too big.

Response Differentiation

It occurs when one response is reinforced, and another is under extinction. I have 2 different behavior topography. It is used in the shaping and differential reinforcement procedure.

E.g., during the pandemic, fist bumps were reinforced, and hugging was put in extinction.

Differential Reinforcement DR (view Task List G-14)

A procedure involving reinforcement + extinction. There are different types:

Differential Reinforcement Of High Rates (DRH)

Reinforcement is provided only if the rate of responses is equal to or higher than a predetermined criterion. It is used to increase the rate of responding.

E.g., if the dog jumps more than 20 hoops in 5min, the reinforcer is delivered.

Differential Reinforcement Of Low Rates (DRL)

Reinforcement is provided only if the rate of responses is equal to or lower than a predetermined criterion. It is used to decrease the rate of responding.

E.g., If the kid raises his hand less than 5 times in 60 min, a reinforcer is delivered.

Differential Reinforcement Of Diminishing Rates (DRD)

Reinforcement is provided only if the rate of responses is equal to or lower than a predetermined criterion, and this criterion gradually decreases over time. It is a progressive DRL schedule, systematically thinning each successive reinforcement opportunity.

Differential Reinforcement Of Paced Responses (DRP)

Reinforcement is based upon the time between responses, only if it is within a specific range. It is DRL+DRH combined; the behavior occurs at no more than and no less than a specific rate.

E.g., playing the piano. Each note must be played within a specific time to produce a song.

Differential Reinforcement Of Incompatible Behavior (DRI)

Reinforcement is provided for a behavior that cannot co-occur with the problem behavior.

E.g., sitting is reinforced and cannot occur simultaneously with running around the room.

Differential Reinforcement Of Other Behavior (DRO)

Deliver reinforcement whenever the problem behavior has not occurred during or at a specific time. Any other behavior can occur except the target behavior.

Differential Reinforcement Of Alternative Behavior (DRA)
Reinforcement is delivered for behavior that is a desirable alternative to the problem behavior but is not necessarily incompatible with it. The alternative behavior is functionally equivalent to the target behavior.
E.g., completing a worksheet is reinforced when behavior targeted for reduction is talk-outs.

Reduce behavior to 0 (zero)	Reduce to appropriate rates of behavior
DRO	DRL
DRI	DRD
DRA	DRP

Lag schedule
Reinforcement for a response is contingent on that response being different from previous responses and some predetermined variables. It is used to increase response variability.
E.g., Lag 3 of praise statements. You get a reinforcement only if your praise is different from the 3 previous ones.

Progressive Schedule of Reinforcement
Systematically thin each successive reinforcement opportunity independent of the client's behavior, until responding stops and reaches the breaking point. This is used to assess the strength of the reinforcer and how far the reinforcer will go. Use for reinforcer assessment and intervention.

Delay to Reinforcement Schedule
The reinforcement is delivered with a delay to teach self-control, FCT, etc.

Compound schedule
Combination of two or more basic schedules and/or differential reinforcement schedules.
7 types:
1)   Concurrent Schedule (conc)
Two or more contingencies of reinforcement occur simultaneously but independently for two or more behaviors. Each schedule is signaled with a different SD. It is a choice so think of the matching law: given 2 choices you will choose to engage in the behavior that has the highest rate of SR in that moment (behavior goes where reinforcement flows).
E.g., If I complete the worksheet, I get a 30sec break. If I spit at the teacher, I get 15min timeout.
2)   Multiple Schedule (mult)
Two or more basic schedules of reinforcement that are alternating and independent of each other, both signaled by a different stimulus. This schedule is associated with behavior contrast effects.
E.g., The tutor Julia signals VR2 for completing math problems at home, and the teacher Camila signals VR10 for completing math problems in class.
E.g.,Traffic light green or red light.

3)   Mixed Schedule (mix)
Two or more basic schedules of reinforcement alternating, without any signaling stimuli and in a random sequence.
This schedule is like the multiple schedule but no SDs.

E.g., RBT Liz sometimes reinforces client behavior with VR5, other times with VR1 or VR8. No signals when she will use one or another.

4)   Chained Schedule (chain)

Two or more basic schedules of reinforcement that are sequentially and in a specific order. Components are signaled, and the reinforcer comes at the end of the sequence.

Each step of the chain serves as an SDs for the next step in the chain.

Each step of the chain serves as a conditioned reinforcer for the previous step in the chain.

E.g., Chiara wants to talk to her best friend on the phone. First, Chiara has to get her phone out of her purse, unlock her phone, and dial her best friend's phone number. After the phone rings and her friend picks up, Chiara can finally say "Hello" and enjoy a conversation with her friend.

5)   Tandem Schedule (tand)

Same as a chained schedule, except it does not use discriminative stimuli with the elements in the chain. It is an unsignaled chain. You need to figure out the sequence trial by error.

E.g., tan FR15/FI2. A student earns a reinforcer after completing 15 math problems, then the first correct response following an elapse of 2min produces reinforcement but they don't know the order of the steps.

6)   Alternative Schedule (alt)

Two or more schedules of reinforcement operate simultaneously, and reinforcement is earned when one of the schedule components is completed. Whichever comes first. It's an either/or schedule that offers a second chance to the learner.

E.g., Get reinforcer whether you complete all 20 questions or if you work on the assignment for 10 minutes.

7)   Conjunctive Schedule (conj)

Two or more schedules of reinforcement operate simultaneously, and reinforcement is earned when both schedule components are completed.

E.g., He gets reinforcement if at least 2min have elapsed and 50 responses have been made. (conj FI2/FR50)

Sd present	Sd Not present	Combine rate and interval
Multiple	Mixed	Alternative
Chained	Tandem	Conjunctive
Concurrent		

Adjunctive Behaviors (AKA: Schedule Induced Behaviors)

Behaviors that occur in between the provision of SR when the SR is not available. Those are time-filling/interim behaviors like smoking, drinking, hair playing, etc.

B-6 Define And Provide Examples Of Positive And Negative Punishment Contingencies

Punishment (AKA: SDP, SP, SD-)

Environmental change that follows a response closely in time, is contingent on that response and decreases the probability of similar responses under similar circumstances.

It is only considered punishment if the behavior decreases in the future! E.g., reprimands are not punishing if the child continues to do the same behavior again in the future.

To identify punishments we can use:

-        Stimulus avoidance assessment: it helps identify stimuli that the client avoids or does not prefer. Those are potential punishers that can be ranked by making "indices of displeasure". Caregivers can help identify those stimuli.

-        Punisher assessment: it determines the effectiveness of the stimuli as punishers.

Note: Threats decrease the behavior in the moment and are not considered punishers.

Important features of the punishment procedure:

• 	Immediacy: deliver punisher immediately after the target behavior
• 	Intensity: start at higher intensity punishers and then decrease gradually over time
• 	Schedule: FR1 schedules are the most effective
• 	Pair with other procedures like DRA, reinforcing alternative behaviors
• 	Make sure the treatment is conducted as planned (treatment integrity)

Positive Punishment (AKA: Type I Punishment)

Adding an aversive stimulus to the environment as the consequence of undesirable behavior, decreases the behavior.

E.g., Being assigned extra training when you break the rules, in the future, you don't break the rules anymore.

Positive Punishment procedures include:

• 	Verbal Reprimands: statement of disapproval contingent on behavior. Mostly common as reprimands, "No", corrective or negative feedback.

E.g., A supervisor conducts an observation of a teacher. The supervisor tells the teacher that their instructional methods were "horrible" and heavily criticized their performance. The teacher no longer uses those instructional methods. The presentation of the verbal reprimand decreased the future frequency of the teacher using those instructional methods.

• 	Restitutional Overcorrection: restore the environment even better than its original state. The topography of the effortful behavior is similar to the problem behavior.

E.g., I throw a piece of paper on the floor, the teacher asks me to pick it up and also clean all the other papers on the floor.

• 	Positive Practice Overcorrection: practice the correct way to engage in the behavior multiple times. The topography of the effortful behavior is the same as the problem behavior.

E.g., I slam the door and RBT asks me to close the door slowly 10 times.

• 	Contingent exercise: the client will engage in exercises not related to the problem behavior.

E.g., Jumping jacks for arriving late at the school game

• 	Response blocking: physically intervening to prevent the completion of the behavior (used for SIB). E.g. client who engages in self-biting is about to bite themselves, they would be physically prevented from doing so.

- Response interruption and redirection (RIRD): variation of response blocking, related to redirecting with vocal/motor response to another activity.

E.g., The client is bubbling and the staff interrupts him by asking multiple questions or singing a preferred song.

- Physical restraint: impede the individual's freedom/movements to keep the client safe
- Contingent aversive stimuli with problem behavior. E.g., Water misting, electric stimulation

Negative Punishment (AKA: Type II Punishment, Penalty Principle, Penalty Contingency)

Removing an appetitive stimulus from the environment as the consequence of undesirable behavior, decreases the behavior.

Some negative procedures include:

- Response Cost (AKA: Penalty): loss of a specific number of positive reinforcers that were already earned, contingent on challenging behavior.

E.g., A fine, removal of tokens

Avoid overuse and consider a possible aggressive response. Plan the amount to be removed in case of challenging behavior, set the rules and deliver the fines immediately and consistently.

- Time out: contingent on challenging behavior, access to specific reinforcers is prohibited for a period of time. Make the time-in environment a good one where the client wants to stay. Explain to the client the rules of the time out and define the behavior that will result in it. Assess the program's effectiveness and set termination criteria. There are different types of time-out procedures:

- Seclusion: the client is placed in a time-out room for a period of time. Most restrictive procedure.

- Exclusionary: client is removed from the time-in setting for a period of time.

- Non-exclusionary: client is not removed from the environment but no involvement is allowed. E.g., The client can only observe without participating. E.g., being on the bench during the game after cursing.

NOTE: time out is not indicated for escape-maintained behavior.

Unwanted Effects Of Punishment

- Avoidance of "punishing agent." Society doesn't like when you use punishing procedures.
- The effects of punishment can be temporary.
- Inappropriate generalization: appropriate responses decreases along with the target behavior
- Aggression could increase
- Emotional responses. The client may try to escape/avoid the practitioner
- The client may imitate your punitive behaviors.
- It requires supervision and training.
- Behavioral contrast: target behavior may decrease in one setting but increase in other
- Recovery from punishment: the rate of behavior temporally increases back to its original state when you interrupt the punishing procedure.

Some ethical considerations regarding the use of punishment procedures are:

- Are we restricting someone else rights?
- Have we tried everything else?
- Is there potential for abuse or overuse?
- Is the procedure legal?
- Is the procedure appropriate for the function of behavior?

B-7 Define And Provide Examples Of Automatic And Socially Mediated Contingencies

Socially Mediated Contingency

The consequence is mediated by the action of another person.

E.g., Rachel's back is itching, and she asks Danielle to scratch it.

Automatic Contingency

The consequence is directly produced by the response. When behavior is evoked, shaped, maintained, or weakened by environmental variables that happen without others' manipulation. In some cases, bodily sensations are considered automatic contingencies like spinning, rocking, and hand-flapping if they reinforce behavior. Note: not all hand flapping is automatic. You can't assume that it has an automatic function, it could also be attention/escape/tangible.

E.g., Hand flapping is the response. The sensation felt increased the hand flapping.

E.g., A patient engages in rocking back and forth on the floor to experience a reduction in anxiety (aversive private event).

Note: Socially mediated and Automatic contingencies apply to all positive/negative reinforcement/punishment.

B-8 Define And Provide Examples Of Unconditioned, Conditioned, And Generalized Reinforcers And Punishers

Unconditioned Reinforcer (AKA: UCR, Primary Reinforcer, Unlearned Reinforcer)

The consequence has the ability to increase the future occurrence of the behavior without prior learning (phylogenic provenance). It requires a state of deprivation to be a reinforcer.

E.g., food, water, sex, regulated body and environmental temperatures.

Unconditioned Punisher (AKA: UCP, Primary Punisher, Unlearned Punisher)

The ability of the stimulus to decrease the future occurrence of the behavior without prior learning (phylogenic provenance).

E.g., extremely hot/cold temperatures, loud noises, painful stimulation, starvation, extreme thirst, and lack of sexual stimulation.

Conditioned Reinforcer (AKA: CR, Secondary Reinforcer, Learned Reinforcer)

A stimulus that initially has no innate reinforcing properties, but acquires reinforcing properties through stimulus-stimulus pairing with unconditioned reinforcers or powerful conditioned reinforcers. Learning history is required so CRs are products of ontogeny.

E.g., praise, toys, high five, candy, etc.

BE CAREFUL: the process occurs through pairing like in respondent conditioning, but the result it's different. With the conditioned reinforcer, a stimulus becomes a reinforcer, with respondent conditioning a neutral stimulus becomes an eliciting antecedent stimulus.

Conditioned Punisher (AKA: CP, Secondary Punisher, Learned Punisher)

A previously neutral stimulus changes that function as a punisher due to prior pairing with one or more other punishers. Learning history is required so they are products of ontogeny.

E.g., One of your colleagues criticized your work performance in front of your friends. When you see her in the staff lunchroom now, you do not enter. This person's presence serves as a conditioned punisher.

Generalized Reinforcer (AKA: GCSR, Nonspecific Reinforcer)

A conditioned reinforcer that has been paired with a variety of other reinforcers and is effective for a wide range of behaviors. It is important to note that the conditioned reinforcer does not have value in its physical properties but in what it represents (i.e., the reinforcers it can be exchanged for). They don't depend on an MO for its effectiveness and they are likely to be reinforcing at any time to anyone. E.g., praise, social attention, etc.

E.g., Money is probably the most widely used generalized conditioned reinforcer in real life. We use the money to buy primary reinforcers such as food and shelter. Children are not born knowing that money is reinforcing; they learn this association over time.

E.g., Tokens are not generalized conditioned reinforcers unless they can be exchanged for something valuable to the person.

Generalized Punisher (AKA: GCSP)

A conditioned punisher that has been paired with a variety of other punishers and is effective for a wide range of behaviors. They are likely to be punishing at any time.

E.g., reprimands like No! or Don't do that! are generalized conditioned punishers for most people because they

Shhh...

have been repeatedly paired with a wide variety of conditioned and unconditioned punishers.
E.g., specific sounds/tastes/visual stimuli, point fines, loss of access, frowns, head shakes, scowls, etc.

	Positive (+)	Negative (-)
Reinforcement (Strengthen)	Positive reinforcement (S^{R+}) Appetitive added (praise, bonus, token, money...)	Negative reinforcement (S^{R-}) Aversive removed (relief from irritant, pain)
Punishment (Weaken)	Positive punishment (S^{P+}) Aversive added (shock, pain, reprimands, "no")	Negative punishment (S^{P-}) Appetitive removed (penalty, loss of privileges/access to preferred activities)

B-9 Define And Provide Examples Of Operant Extinction
view Task List G-15

Extinction

It is defined as the process of withholding reinforcement for a previously reinforced behavior that decreases the rate of that behavior. This means that learned behaviors will gradually disappear if they are not reinforced. Important features:

•   History of reinforcement required. Extinction is more rapid if the behavior was previously reinforced in a continuous schedule (CRF). Behaviors reinforced with a variable intermittent schedule (VR/VI) are more resistant to EXT.

•   Not adding or removing anything, but withholding.

•   Combining EXT with other procedures is suggested.

•   Always provide a replacement behavior with the same function as the behavior being put on extinction.

•   Plan for maintenance

•   Let the behavior happen but do not reinforce it (this is not response blocking)

Do NOT use:

•   If the behavior can cause harm or it's too dangerous

•   If the behavior needs to decrease quickly

•   If withholding the reinforcement is not always possible. Consistency is essential for this procedure!

•   Others may imitate the disruptive behavior.

Extinction Procedures

1)   Behaviors maintained by Positive Reinforcement (Attention/tangibles)

- When problem behavior occurs, withhold attention (ignore).

- Wait for a period of calm without problem behavior

- Deliver attention to appropriate responses that you can prompt

Note that attention behaviors include: reprimands, eye contact, talking to the client, making mean comments, etc. E.g., A client engages in disruptive classroom behavior (e.g., yelling in class) and no one is reacting to his yelling. If the client stops yelling and uses functional communication to get attention, the teacher/instructor will give attention immediately.

For tangibles, the procedure is the same, but we withhold the item/activity when problem behavior occurs.

2)   Behaviors maintained by Negative Reinforcement (Escape extinction)

- The problem behavior does not produce a removal of the aversive stimulus. The person cannot escape from the aversive situation, most often a demand.

- Guide the individual through the task if necessary

- Wait for the individual to complete the task before allowing escape

3)   Behaviors maintained by Automatic Reinforcement (Sensory extinction)

- Masking or removing the sensory consequence. E.g., if a person bites his lip, put a lip balm to remove the sensation

- More difficult to manage because we don't know what is reinforcing the behavior. Is it the touch? The sound? The light?

Unwanted Effects Of Extinction

1)   Extinction Burst

An immediate increase in the response frequency/force/magnitude after removing the positive, negative or automatic reinforcement. The intensity of the extinction burst could be high, and it could be unethical and dangerous to put behavior on extinction. Always plan for extinction bursts and spontaneous recovery. Ignore the behavior but not the child! The safety of our clients is always a priority

E.g., A vending machine that does not deliver a soda after you have paid and pushed the button. In previous experience, putting in money and pressing the button provided the soda. This behavior has a strong history of reinforcement. When the situation changes and the soda machine stops delivering the soda, the reaction is to push the buttons madly. The mad button-pushing is the extinction burst. After this, the button-pushing behavior is decreased and then stops.

2)   Response Variation

New responses emerge after removing the positive, negative or automatic reinforcement.

Some may be appropriate, and some not.

3)   Initial Increase In Response Magnitude

Increase the intensity/volume/duration/force of behavior following the extinction procedure.

E.g., The scream gets louder after removing attention as a reinforcer.

4)   Spontaneous Recovery

The reappearance of the behavior after its frequency has decreased or stopped altogether. It is only for a limited period if the extinction procedure is still in place.

5)   Resurgence

The reappearance of a behavior that was placed on extinction, after a second behavior is placed on extinction too.

E.g., The child screams (B1) for attention from the teacher, this behavior is ignored, and attention is provided only when the child uses his inside voice (B2). After some time, the teacher stops attending to the child when he's using his inside voice (B2 extinction), so the screaming (B1) resumes. If the replacement behavior was FCT training and the client's functional communication is not being honored, they may use the problem behavior again to try to access reinforcement.

6)   Emotional Outbursts And Aggression

The appearance of behaviors, such as hitting, property damage, and crying, could be evoked by extinction.

7)   Behavioral Contrast (view Task List H-5).

E.g., Mom ignores spitting, so the child's behavior decreases (EXT). Dad continues to provide reprimands when the child spits (Positive Reinforcement), so the spitting increases.

8)   Unintentional EXT of Desired Behaviors

Extinction is different from:

	What is this procedure?	Vs Extinction
Ignoring	Ignore the behavior	Ignoring is considered Ext only if the function is attention.
NCR	NCR decrease behavior by changing antecedents	Ext decrease behavior by changing consequences
Response blocking	Response blocking prevents the response from occurring, it is blocked.	In Ext the behavior can still occur but we withhold the reinforcement.
Respondent EXT	Respondent Ext is unpairing of CS and US. The CS returns a neutral stimulus.(Pavlov)	Operant Ext is withholding reinforcement (consequence) when the behavior occurs.

B-10 Define And Provide Examples Of Stimulus Control

Stimulus Control

The presence or absence of an antecedent stimulus alters the dimension of a specific behavior. Behavior that occurs more often in the presence of an SD than in its absence is said to be under stimulus control.

Stimulus discrimination training entails reinforcing responses in the presence of an SD and not reinforcing responses in the presence of the S-Delta.

E.g. the TV(SD) signals the availability of watching a new tv show, while a book (S∆) doesn't produce the reinforcement of watching a tv show.

SD: Discriminative Stimulus For Reinforcement

An antecedent stimulus that evokes a specific behavior due to a history of reinforcement in the presence of that antecedent stimulus. The signal tells you that reinforcement is available.

E.g., the sight of the Exit sign is the SD for finding a way to leave the room.

S-delta (S∆): Discriminative Stimulus For Extinction (No Reinforcement Available)

An antecedent stimulus that abates a specific behavior due to a history of no reinforcement in the presence of that antecedent stimulus.

E.g., having the wrong key is the S∆ for opening the door.

SDP: Discriminative Stimulus For Punishment

An antecedent stimulus that abates a specific behavior due to a history of punishment in the presence of that antecedent stimulus.

E.g., the sight of a police car is an SDP for speeding.

S-Delta P (S∆P): Discriminative Stimulus For Recovery (No Punishment)

An antecedent stimulus that evokes a specific behavior due to a history of no punishment in the presence of that antecedent stimulus.

E.g., an empty highway in the desert evokes driving over the speed limit.

	Reinforcement	Punishment
Correlated with Past **Availability**	SD Evokes behavior	SDP Abates behavior
Correlated with Past **Non- Availability**	S∆ Abates behavior	S∆P Evokes behavior

Faulty Stimulus Control

Occurs when a behavior comes under the restricted control of an irrelevant antecedent stimulus.

Overselective Stimulus Control

The range of discriminative stimuli features controlling the behavior is extremely limited.

E.g., focus on one feature of an object other than the entire object itself.

Stimulus Salience

It refers to how obvious or prominent a stimulus is in a person's environment. If a person has visual deficits, then the visual stimulus will not have as much salience as the auditory stimulus, for example. In order to notice a stimulus, and for that stimulus to have salience, a learner must possess pre-attending skills necessary for the setting.

Masking (Stimulus Blocking)

It occurs when the salience of a stimulus is decreased. A competing stimulus blocks the evocative power of the stimulus, decreasing its effectiveness. There is in fact stimulus control but the subject is unable to perform the skill.

E.g., a child knows how to play piano in the living room of his house, but in a big concert full of people, he chokes and cannot play the song.

E.g., I answer the phone when I am available, but right now the dinner is burning in the oven so I don't answer it.

Overshadowing

It occurs when the first stimulus has no more stimulus control and interferes with the acquisition (distractors).

E.g., the child is in a piano class but the environment is loud with other people playing other instruments and the child cannot learn the material because of the competing stimuli.

In order to reduce the effect of overshadowing and masking, we must apply antecedent interventions such as: arranging the environment to reduce "noise" from the unwanted stimulus, making the instructional stimuli intense, and consistently reinforcing behavior in the presence of the desired stimulus.

B-11 Define And Provide Examples Of Discrimination, Generalization, And Maintenance
(View Task List G-21, G-22)

Generalization
The extent to which a learner emits the target behavior in a setting or stimulus situation that is different from the instructional setting. The greater the generalization, the less the discrimination.
Generality is one of the seven dimensions of behavior analysis and it is a necessity because we can't teach every single behavior in every circumstance.
There are 2 types of generalization:

1)   Stimulus Generalization
The spread of training effects to stimuli not present during training. The behavior is the same in different situations not trained.
It is the extent to which stimuli, other than the SD, acquire stimulus control over the behavior.
It is a loose degree of stimulus control, the opposite of stimulus discrimination (which indicates a tight degree of control).
E.g., teach to say "Hi" when seeing different people.
E.g., the child was potty trained at home and now he uses the toilet even at his grandma's house.
E.g., a client is able to label a 2D picture of a dog and then sees a real dog walking on the street and is able to label that dog.

Overgeneralization
It's an incorrect or inappropriate stimulus generalization.
E.g., teach to say "Daddy" when seeing the father, but the kid also says it for all other adult males. (not good!)
E.g., prejudice against certain races or ethnicities

2)   Response Generalization (AKA: Response Induction)
Spread of training effects to untrained responses that are functionally equivalent to the trained target behavior. A new behavior is developed in the same situation. Induction means the introduction of novel responses.
E.g., the child learned to say "Hi" when seeing mom, he also says "Hello", "good morning" and "bye" without training.

How do you know if it's response or stimulus generalization?
If the response/behavior changes in the example, then it is a response generalization.
Plan for Generalization:
1.   Train and hope (not really a strategy)
2.   Sequential modification: assess if generalization occurs, if not then train. It's not a proactive approach.
3.   Introducing to natural contingencies: select behaviors that are likely to be reinforced in the natural environment. (Relevance of Behavior Rule)
4.   Multiple Exemplar Training: train enough and relevant response/stimulus exemplars but not every single one. E.g., teach to eat with a fork and chopstick.
E.g., teach to write with different pens, but not all pens.
5.   Train Loosely: vary the Non-critical stimuli. E.g., the tone of voice, words used, time of the day, room, different staff, etc.

6.   Indiscriminable Contingency: the client can't discriminate if the next response will provide the reinforcement. Vary the schedule of the reinforcement, use delay and thin the schedule over time.

7.   Program Common Stimuli: import some stimuli from the natural environment to the training setting. Ensure some SDs exist both in the instructional and generalization setting. E.g., train at home with the client to tolerate a dental procedure. Use the same dentist's chair and the same tools that the client will find during the dentist appointment.

8.   Train then place: first train, then bring the client to the natural environment

9.   Train in place: bring the client to the natural environment and train

10.   Mediate generalization: arrange people or things to act as a medium for the transfer of the behavior from the training setting to the natural environment. E.g., ask people to reinforce your correct behavior, use an agenda/planner,

11.   Self Management: teach the client self-management behaviors to enable them to manage the target behavior on their own. E.g., Self-recording, self-rule.

12.   Negative Teaching Examples: teach the client to discriminate the settings, times, and conditions in which it is not appropriate to display a certain behavior. It is used to promote discrimination and stimulus control. E.g., you can say dirty jokes with your friends but not with your boss.

13.   General Case Analysis: teach your client all the different stimulus variations and response variations they may come across in the generalization setting, and teach all the similarities and differences. E.g., I teach Sam to use all the different types of Air fryers that exist.

14.   Train to generalize: reinforce generalization when it happens

Discrimination

Discrimination training occurs when behavior is reinforced in one environment and not in another. This means teaching a client how to tell the difference between two or more stimuli. The behavior is the same for both stimuli. E.g., teach to say "Daddy" only when seeing the father and not other males. (St. Discrimination)
E.g., Hugging is reinforced at home but put on extinction at the mall.
(Note: view Differentiation for difference)

Maintenance

The extent to which a learner continues to perform the target behavior after a portion or all the intervention responsible for the behavior's initial appearance in the learner's repertoire has been terminated.

Important differences:

Stimulus Discrimination	Response Differentiation
2 different stimuli S1-S2	2 different behaviors B1-B2
S1-R-EXT	B1-EXT
S2-R-Reinforcement	B2-Reinforcement

Stimulus Discrimination	Stimulus Generalization
Narrow/tight stimulus control	Loose stimulus control
E.g., I call my mom "Mommy", but not other women.	E.g., I refer to ALL females as "women".

B-12 Define And Provide Examples Of Motivating Operations

Motivating Operations (MO)

An antecedent environmental variable that increases or decreases the effectiveness of a consequence (value-altering effect) and thus evokes or abates a response (behavior-altering effect).

It's what you care about at this moment in time.

Do I care about the consequence offered? (value-altering): Establishing or Abolishing Operation

Am I going to do something to get it? (behavior-altering): Evoke or Abate behavior

2 types of MO:

1.   Establishing Operation (EO) for Reinforcement

•   Value-altering effect: Establishing effect. Increases the current effectiveness of some stimulus, object, or event as reinforcement in the moment. An item can become more valuable when it is needed.

E.g., water becomes more valuable as you continue to eat more and more salty food.

E.g., food deprivation increases the value of food.

•   Behavior-altering effect: Evocative effect. Increases in the frequency of the behavior in the moment. You engage in the behavior that gives you the reinforcer you want.

This can be used in direct work with a client by limiting access to highly preferred items (e.g., limiting the time they spend on an iPad) to ensure that these items become highly motivating and maintain their value as reinforcers.

2.   Abolishing Operation (AO) for Reinforcement

•   Value-altering effect: Abolishing effect. Decreases the current effectiveness of some stimulus, object, or event as reinforcement. An item can become less valuable when you have too much of it.

E.g., sleep becomes less motivating after a full night's rest.

E.g., satiation decreases the value of food.

•   Behavior-altering effect: Abative effect. Decreases in the frequency of the behavior in the moment. You don't engage in the behavior for something you don't want.

When thinking about direct work with a client, edible reinforcers are likely to not be effective immediately after the client eats a meal. Or a client may not be motivated to work for an iPad if they have been on the iPad for the last several hours.

Function-Altering Effect

MOs typically effect behavior in the moment but they can also give us an opportunity to evoke a new response and change future behavior. We have a function-altering effect when a consequence for a behavior in the presence of an MO changes the behavior in the future.

Four-term contingency: MO – SD – R – SR+

	Reinforcement	Punishment
EO	Evoke bx	Abate bx
AO	Abate bx	Evoke bx

E.g., AO for punishment decreases the value of punishment as a consequence (punishment is less effective) and evokes behavior.

E.g., EO for punishment increase the value of punishment as a consequence and abates behavior to terminate it.

Unconditioned Motivating Operations (UMO)

A type of MOs that have a value-altering effect due to phylogenic provenance (genetic). It does not require a history of learning for the item to have reinforcement values.

E.g., if a person has been up for 20 hours straight, sleep becomes more motivating.

The main types of UMO are: deprivation and satiation (food, water, activity, sleep, oxygen, sex), temperature regulation (too hot/too cold), and painful stimulus (onset/magnification).

Conditioned Motivating Operations (CMO)

A type of MOs that have a value-altering effect on other stimuli due to ontogenic provenance (learning history). The CMO changes the frequency of the behavior associated with those other stimuli in the moment.

E.g, having the phone dead, makes the charges more valuable as a reinforcer and in the moment the behavior of looking for a charger is increased.

There are 3 types of CMOS:

1. CMO-S (Surrogate MO)

An antecedent stimulus or condition acquires its value-altering and behavior-altering effects through pairing with another motivating operation. A pairing process needs to take place and the neutral stimulus becomes the CMO-S.

E.g., food deprivation is been paired with the sight of the clock at 12pm. Now, when I see it's 12pm, it increases the value of food as reinforcers and evokes making a sandwich even when not hungry.

The clock is the CMO-S.

E.g., I see the ketchup and I want the fries.

E.g, I go to the movie and I want popcorn.

E.g., I see it's snowing so I wear warm clothes.

2. CMO-R (Reflexive MO)

An antecedent stimulus or condition that establishes or abolishes its own termination as an effective form of negative reinforcement.

Increase the value of escape and avoidance: Escape from pain, Avoidance with a warning signal.

The warning of the pain is the CMO-R.

E.g., I pair an alarm with the delivery of a shock in a rat box. The rat behavior of pressing the lever removes the shock. After repeated trials, the alarm is the CMO-R/the warning stimulus that evokes the behavior of pressing the lever to avoid the shock/painful stimulation.

E.g., The teacher said "Start the assignment" and that serves as a warning signal that increases the behavior of escape due to the difficulty of the work.

3. CMO-T (Transitive MO)

An antecedent stimulus that establishes or abolishes the effectiveness of a second stimulus as a reinforcer and evokes or abates behavior that has been reinforced by the second stimulus in the past.

To get from here to there, you need something else, a tool. Previously neutral stimuli are now reinforcers for the client because something is blocking access to the conditioned reinforcer and problem-solving behaviors are needed.

E.g., The beer and the bottle opener. The sealed bottle is the CMO-T. The bottle opener is the conditioned Sr+

whose value it's increased and is the solution to the problem.

E.g., the sight of sashimi on the plate is the CMO-T for chopsticks, which increased his value as a reinforcer.

E.g., charger for your phone, spoon for your soup, straw for your drink, etc.

B-13 Define And Provide Examples Of Rule-Governed And Contingency-Shaped Behavior
View Task List G-6

B-14 Define And Provide Examples Of The Verbal Operants

view Task List G-11

Verbal Behavior

Verbal behavior is behavior that is reinforced through the mediation of another person's behavior. It is defined by the function of the response, rather than its form. Language involves an interaction between 2 roles that alternate constantly:

- The speaker: emits any verbal behavior, in any form, and he/she gains access to reinforcement
- The listener: serves as an audience, provides reinforcers for the speaker, and responds in specific ways to the speaker's behavior.

Verbal behavior is not only spoken words but also sign language, braille, icon selection, facial expressions, and fingerspelling.

The basic components of a speaker's verbal repertoire are called elementary verbal operants:

Mand

A type of verbal operant in which a speaker asks for what he needs or wants. It's under the functional control of Mos and has a history of specific reinforcement.

E.g., Alex asks for water by saying, "Can I have water?". The MO is being thirsty.

Other examples of mands are Extended mand:

• Magical mand: the reinforcer will not be delivered even if you ask multiple times. E.g., I wish I had a million dollars.

• Superstitious mand: reinforcer is sometimes delivered accidentally. E.g., I won the game while wearing my lucky red underwear.

Tact

A type of verbal operant in which the speaker names things and actions that the speaker has direct contact with through any of the sense modes. It is under the control of a non-verbal stimulus. Also called labeling or naming. The learner labels something within their environment.

E.g. Jane sees a clock in her classroom and says "A clock!".

During training the instructor can use the prompt "what's this?" after showing an object. The goal of training is that the client will emit Pure Tacts where only a non-verbal SD controls the response.

• Generic tact extension: This happens when a novel stimulus shares some of the defining features of a familiar stimulus. For example, a child is able to label a picture of a car and able to label a real car when outside.

• Metaphorical tact extension: This happens when a novel stimulus has some similarities to a familiar stimulus but is missing defining features. For example, a person saying their coffee is as cold as ice. This is only a metaphor for their coffee being likely at room temperature.

• Metonymical tact extension: This happens when a novel stimulus accidentally gets paired with another stimulus and overgeneralizes. For example, a child labels a cat based on its four legs but then labels a dog, goat and cow all as a cat because they all have 4 legs.

• Solecistic tact extension: This is a poor use of grammar/sentence structure to label something. For example, a child who says "me tired" instead of "I am tired."

We can also tact private events like nausea, pain, and sickness, and it is accomplished through two methods:
- Public Accomplishment: observable stimulus accompanies private behavior. E.g., See the child being hit by a ball

in the face. We assume he's in pain, and we can tell him, "that hurts!".

- Collateral Response: observable behavior that reliably occurs with private stimuli. E.g., we didn't see the ball hit the child, but we observed him holding his head and crying. Those behaviors inform us that he must feel pain.

Duplic
The speaker repeats the verbal behavior of another speaker, duplicate. A verbal discriminative stimulus controls it with point-to-point correspondence and formal similarity with the response.
- Echoic: I say "cookie," and you repeat "cookie."
- Mimetic: I sign the ASL sign for "cookie," and you sign the ASL sign for "cookie."
- Copying a text: I write "cookie," and you write "cookie."

Codic
Verbal behavior that has NO formal similarity to the stimulus that preceded it but has point-to-point correspondence.

– Textual (from written to spoken of the exact words): I see the written word "boy," and I say "boy." It is reading out loud or in your head.

– Transcription/Dictating (from spoken to written of the exact words): the teacher says, "Biden is the president," and I wrote in my notebook, "Biden is the president."

Intraverbal
A verbal response that does not have formal similarity nor point-to-point correspondence. It's a typical form of conversation, answering personal or WH questions, fill-ins, and songs.

E.g., the teacher asks, "What color is your lunchbox?" John responds, "Red."

E.g., the mom says "the wheels on the bus go..." and the child answers "round and round."

Listener Responding (AKA: Receptive Behavior)
The learner responds to the request of another person in the form of action. Not verbal behavior but simply following directions.

E.g., Kyle's friend says "high five!" and Kyle gives him a high five.

E.g., I say "close the door," and my husband closes it.

Motor Imitation
The learner copies the movement of another person.

E.g., Sasha's therapist says, "Copy me!" and then the therapist stomps his feet. Sasha stomps her feet.

Match-to-Sample (VPMTS)
The learner sorts and matches like items.

E.g., Theresa's dad says, "Match" and hands her a picture of a door. Theresa then matches this picture to an identical picture of a door.

Autoclitic

It's a secondary verbal operant, it doesn't occur on its own. It's verbal behavior that modifies a primary verbal behavior to benefit the listener, add more info, comment, and clarify. Autoclitics can include gestures, tone of voice, prepositions, words, and facial expressions.

E.g., I think, I guess, I'm sure,...

E.g., I don't want, I really want,...

E.g., One ball, Green ball, 3 balls,...
- Autoclitic Mand: add supplemental control by a related MO.

E.g., Don't be offended, but I'm not hungry.
- Autoclitic Tact: controlled by some nonverbal aspect of the main response.

E.g., I know I left the keys at home.

Antecedent	Formal Similarity	Point to point correspondence	Verbal Behavior	Consequence
MO	n/a	n/a	Mand	Specific reinforcer
Nonverbal SD	n/a	n/a	Tact	Generalized reinforcer
Verbal SD	Y	Y	Duplic - Echoic - Mimetic - Copying text	Generalized reinforcer
Verbal SD	N	Y	Codic - Textual - Transcription	Generalized reinforcer
Verbal SD	N	N	Intraverbal	Generalized reinforcer

B-15 Define And Provide Examples Of Derived Stimulus Relations

view Task List G-12

Frame

The frame is a stimulus relation between two or more stimuli that function within that class. Framing is a behavior of making those relational connections, and it is learned.

Derived Stimulus Relations

Learning one aspect of something, automatically teaches you something new. It's the emergence of untrained derived relations between stimuli due to sameness, differences, comparisons, etc., to train relations.

3 types:

1)   Reflexivity

A type of stimulus-to-stimulus relation in which the learner, without any prior training or reinforcement for doing so, selects a comparison stimulus that is the same as the

sample stimulus. A=A

E.g., the sample stimulus is a picture of a tree, and the three comparison stimuli are a picture of a mouse, a cookie, and a duplicate of the tree picture used as the sample stimulus. The learner selects the picture of the tree without a history of reinforcement for making the tree-picture-to-tree-picture match.

2)   Symmetry

A type of stimulus-to-stimulus relationship in which the learner, without prior training or reinforcement for doing so, demonstrates the reversibility of matched sample and comparison

stimuli. A = B trained, then B = A not trained.

E.g., If a learner is taught when presented with a picture of grapes (sample stimulus A) to

select the written word grapes (sample stimulus B). When presented with the written word grapes (sample stimulus B), without additional training or reinforcement, the learner selects the picture of grapes (sample stimulus A).

3)   Transitivity

An untrained stimulus-stimulus relation that emerges as a product of training two other stimulus-stimulus relations. A = B, and B = C are trained, then A = C is derived.

E.g., If you say Bird and show a child a picture of a bird, then you show a picture of a bird and match it to a real bird in a cage, the relationship between saying bird and the caged animal is acquired.

Coffee and Notes:

C. Measurement, Data Display, and Interpretation

C-1:   Establish operational definitions of behavior.

C-2:   Distinguish among direct, indirect, and product measures of behavior.

C-3:   Measure occurrence (e.g., frequency, rate, percentage).

C-4:   Measure temporal dimensions of behavior (e.g., duration, latency, interresponse time).

C-5:   Measure form and strength of behavior (e.g., topography, magnitude).

C-6:   Measure trials to criterion.

C-7:   Design and implement sampling procedures (i.e., interval recording, time sampling).

C-8:   Evaluate the validity and reliability of measurement procedures.

C-9:   Select a measurement system to obtain representative data given the dimentions of behavior and the logistics of observing and recording.

C-10:   Graph data to communicate relevant quantitative relations (e.g., equal-Interval graphs, bar graphs, cumulative records).

C-11:   Interpret graphed data. Distinguish between dependent and independent variables.

C-1 Establish Operational Definitions Of Behavior

Behavior is anything a person does, that can be observed, repeated, or measured.

A good rule of thumb is always to describe behavior so that someone completely unfamiliar with the client would be able to take over the data collection just by reading the description. Therefore, target behaviors must be explicitly defined as operational definitions.

Characteristics of an operational definition:

• Objective: the behavior is observable and can be recorded reliably by others.

• Clear: readable and unambiguous, allows for replication. (Technological dimension of ABA)

• Complete: boundaries are defined with examples and non-examples, what is included and excluded.

Defining target behavior 2 types:

• Function-based definitions: identify responses as members of the targeted response class solely by their common effect on the environment. The outcome of the behavior is the most important.

• Topography-based definitions: identify responses by the shape or form of the behavior, how does the behavior look like.

Note: using examples and non-examples, the onset/offset of the behavior will strengthen a behavioral definition.

Non-example of Tantrum behavior: getting extremely worked up and frustrated, yelling or crying.

E.g., of Tantrum behavior: Any instance of kicking, dropping to the ground, banging head on the floor, or crying with or without tears for at least 30sec. The behavior stops after 1min of termination of the previously mentioned behavior. It does not include dropping to the ground during play activities.

E.g., Face hitting: open-hand or closed-hand contact with the face or head; this does not include instances where the client rubs the face or places her head in her hands.

C-2 Distinguish Among Direct, Indirect, And Product Measures Of Behavior

Measurement

Quantifying objects, events, or behavior. Characteristics of measures:

- Standard: used by the community
- Absolute: the measure never changes
- Universal: can be applied to every instance

Direct Measure

Measurement in which the behavior being measured is the actual behavior of interest.

- Behavior is measured as it is occurring, when it is happening
- More valid
- Does not require inference

E.g., observe and record data on the number of phone calls made in a day, duration of each call, the time between calls, the time you pick up the phone.

Indirect Measure

Measurement in which the behavior is not measured as it is happening. It is considered less valid than direct measurement because there are interferences between the data obtained and the actual behavior of interest.

- Interviews
- Surveys
- Questionnaires
- Rating scales

E.g., Customer satisfaction

E.g., Asking a parent about their child's behavior using rating scales and interviews.

E.g., Using a Standardized test as an indicator of mastery

Product Measures

Measuring a change in the environment produced by behavior that lasts long enough for measurement to take place. The measurement occurs after the behavior took place. Mostly used when we cannot observe behavior in real time. (E.g., it is happening at night and sessions occur during the day). It is only possible if each occurrence of the target behavior produces the same permanent product and the permanent product can only be produced by the target behavior.

- Natural (anything left from the behavior that occurred)
- Contrived (audio/video recording)

Good measure because:

- The practitioner can do something else
- Measurement may be more accurate
- Facilitates data collection for IOA and treatment integrity
- Enables measurement of complex behaviors and multiple response class
- No reactivity

E.g., Counting the number of cigarettes in an ashtray.

E.g., Counting the number of worksheets completed at the end of the day.

E.g., 2 margaritas ready to drink at the bar.

E.g., An empty dishwasher.

Continuous Methods Of Recording

Continuous Methods capture all instances of behavior during the observation period. 4 types:

- Event recording: Count, rate, celeration. Used with behavior that has a clear beginning and end.
- Latency recording
- IRT recording
- Duration recording

C-3 Measure Occurrence (E.g., Frequency, Rate, Percentage)

Dimensional Quantities
A measurable aspect of a fundamental property of behavior. They are: count, rate, celeration, IRT, latency, and duration.

Count (AKA: Frequency)
The number of times a behavior occurs. No time is given.
E.g., 10 jumps
E.g., 10 candies in the jar

Rate
The number of responses per unit of time. Count/time. Typically reported as per minute, hour, day, week, month. Used for free operant behaviors, do not use for DTT or for continuous behaviors.
E.g., 10 jumps in 5 min
E.g., 3 hits/1 hour

Celeration
Change in rate of response over time. Rate/time. Behavior can accelerate (go faster) or decelerate (go slower) over time. It is associated with fluency building and the use of the Standard Celeration Chart.
E.g., the first day the child screams 5times/1hour. On the second day, he screams 10times/1hour. The screaming is accelerating across sessions.

Repeatability		Temporal Locus	Temporal Extent
Count	Rate, IRT, Celeration	Latency	Duration

- Repeatability (AKA Event Recording) = behavior can occur repeatedly through time. (Count, rate, IRT, Celeration). It is used for discrete behaviors that have a clear start and end points.
- Temporal Locus= behavior occurs at a certain point in time with respect to other events (Latency, rate, IRT, Celeration)
- Temporal Extent= every instance of behavior occurs during some amount of time (Duration)

Derivative Measures
Data obtained from direct measures of behavior. These are: percentages and trials to criterion (view Task List C-6).

Percentage (AKA: Percent of Occurrence)
The percentage of occurrence is a derivative measure of target responses over the total number of opportunities. One limitation of this measurement is that if too few opportunities are provided in which the individual can respond, the data will not be accurate as the individual is not able to respond.
E.g., Charlie responded to his name during 4 out of 10 trials, therefore his percent of occurrence was 40%.

C-4 Measure Temporal Dimensions Of Behavior (E.g., Duration, Latency, Inter-Response Time)

Duration (AKA: Temporal Extent)
The total amount of time in which a behavior occurs from start to end. Used for behavior that occur for a long period of time. It can be calculated for the total duration per session or duration per occurrence.
E.g., The child cried for 20 min (single instance of behavior).
E.g., The child cried for 1 h in total during the session (15min+30min+15min=1h total).

Latency (AKA: Response Latency)
The measure of time between the antecedent stimulus and the response. It is used to look at how much time passes when there is an opportunity to emit the behavior. The primary concern is in latency that are too long or too short.
E.g., The child started screaming 30sec after the parents said "No".
E.g., The time between the question and the answer
E.g., The time between the fire alarm and total evacuation of the building

Inter-Response Time (IRT)
The measure of time between two consecutive responses. There is an inverse relationship between rate and IRT:
- Short IRT: high rates of responding
- Long IRT: low rates of responding
Measure IRT when the time between responses needs to be increased or reduced. It is used in DRL and DRH procedures.
E.g., Eating too fast or too slow, you record the time between each bite to reduce or increase it.
E.g., The child screams 2 min after the last time he screamed.

C-5 Measure Form And Strength Of Behavior (E.g., Topography, Magnitude)

Topography (AKA: Form)

The physical form or shape of the behavior. How does the behavior look like?

E.g., Ring the doorbell: Use the index finger to press the doorbell button.

Topographies can be different but have the same form.

E.g., touching mom's shoulder and screaming "Mom!" have the same function of getting mom's attention, but they are in different forms.

Magnitude (AKA: Strength, Force, Intensity, Severity)

The size, force, or intensity with which a response is emitted.

E.g., Screaming vs. whispering.

E.g., Aggression: a light push may be a low-intensity behavior, whereas a full-force shove knocking a person over would be a high-intensity behavior. Both would be considered aggression but happening at different intensities.

C-6 Measure Trials To Criterion

Trials To Criterion

A measure of the number of response opportunities needed to achieve a targeted level of performance. It is the criterion of success and it is set from the beginning.

Used to compare the efficiency of treatment and assess skill acquisition.

E.g., the learner will take data on solving division problems until he can solve 20 problems in 10 min or less. How many trials did it take to reach that goal?

E.g., it took 20 trials to master imitation of clap hands.

C-7 Design And Implement Sampling Procedures (E.g., Interval Recording, Time Sampling)

Interval Recording (AKA: Time Sampling, Discontinuous Measurement)

Not all instances of behavior are captured during the observation period. The measurement gives an estimate/ sample of the behavior.

The observation period is divided into smaller time periods, and criteria for occurrence or nonoccurrence are established.

Data are typically reported as a percentage of intervals.

Use for continuous or high-rate behaviors. Do not use for infrequent behaviors.

There are 3 forms of time sampling procedures:

1.   Partial Interval Recording (PIR)

Interval recording in which occurrence is noted if the behavior occurs at any time during the interval. "Did the behavior occur at all during the time interval?"

The interval must be short typically 5/15 sec.

- •   Mark + as soon as the behavior occurs during the interval
- •   Mark – at the end of the interval if behavior did not occur at all

Partial-interval recording is not concerned with how many times the behavior occurred during the interval or how long the behavior was present, just that it occurred at some point during the interval.

It overestimates the duration of the behavior during the observation period.

It is used for behavior targeted for decrease.

2.   Whole Interval Recording (WIR)

Interval recording in which occurrence is only noted if the behavior occurs for the entire interval. "Did the behavior occur during the whole time interval?"

The interval must be short typically 5/15 sec.

- •   Mark - as soon as the behavior stops occurring.
- •   Mark + at the end of the interval if behavior did occur the entire interval

It underestimates the duration of responding. It is used only for behavior targeted for increase and that have a significant duration.

3.   Momentary Time Sampling (MTS)

Interval recording in which the occurrence or nonoccurrence of behavior is recorded at the end of the interval. "Is the behavior occurring at this point in time?"

- •   Mark + if the behavior is occurring at the end of the interval
- •   Mark – if the behavior is not occurring at the end of the interval

It is very easy to record and it is used when the observer has a lot of other responsibilities (E.g., teachers). It may not be representative of the behavior. Do not use for low count or short duration behaviors.

Planned Activity Check (PLACHECK)

Variation of MTS where the total number of members of a group engaging in the target behavior is noted at the end of the interval. The data is the number of people or % of individuals engaging in the targeted behavior.

C-8 Evaluate The Validity And Reliability Of Measurement Procedures

There are 3 indicators of trustworthy measurement:

1) Validity

Correspondence of a measure to behavior legitimately and directly measured. It's the most important of the indicators: without validity, accuracy and reliability have no value.

Validity involves the extent to which the data represents the phenomenon being assessed, they should be representative and measured in the condition of interest. Are you measuring the right thing?

E.g., If you want to reduce your weight, measuring the time you spend at the gym is not representative. We should measure the actual weight using a scale. (relevant dimension)

E.g., you want to measure occurrences of tantrums in the morning before going to school. You take data in the afternoon and the data shows 0 occurrences, but the data is not valid because it was not taken in the condition of interest.

2) Accuracy

Comparison of a measure with a known standard.

Accuracy refers to the extent to which the observed value matches a true value.

Does the data match what actually occurred? What you measured is what, in fact, happened.

If true values can't be established, rely on reliability measures.

3) Reliability

Consistency of measurement. Reliability involves the stability of the methods used to obtain the data. It's the degree to which repeating a measurement procedure produces the same result, we can use IOA to compare data between 2 or more observers.

Will repeated measures yield consistent data?

Reliable data doesn't always mean accurate data or valid data.

Interobserver Agreement (IOA)

It's the empirical and most common way of measuring integrity in ABA.

Two or more observers take data on the same treatment or event, independent of each other but using the same measurement system, then they compare their observed values. IOA is reported in % and it should be collected for 25% of sessions. The goal is to reach 100% IOA but at least 80% is considered acceptable.

We want the IOA to be as higher as possible: high IOA=high believability.

Use IOA to:

- Assess staff competence
- Identify observer drift
- Confirms if the variability of data is not due to who was recording the data but only to actual changes in behavior
- Confirms if the measurement system is easy or too difficult to follow

There are different methods for calculating IOA:

- Repeatability Measure IOA
- Temporal/Duration IOA

- Time Sampling Procedure IOA

Repeatability Measure IOA

1.   **Total Count IOA**: is the percentage of agreement regarding the total number of responses.

Formula: (smaller count/larger count) *100

E.g., Observer A: 3 instances of behavior, Observer B: 5 instances of behavior.
IOA= 3/5 *100= 60% IOA

2.   **Mean Count Per Interval IOA**: it is used to calculate the agreement between the count of the 2 observers within each interval.
Break up the observation into intervals. Calculate the total count IOA for each interval. Add up that IOA for all intervals and divide by the total number of intervals.

Formula: (Int1 IOA+ Int2 IOA + ...) / Tot. # of intervals

Interval	Observer A	Observer B	Total count IOA
1	4	3	¾ *100= 75%
2	1	2	½ * 100= 50%
3	5	5	5/5 *100= 100%

Mean count IOA: 75% + 50% + 100%= 225%/3= 75% IOA

3.   **Exact Count Per Interval IOA**: it's the most strict method. Percentage of intervals in which observers recorded the same count (100% IOA).

Formula: (Exact IOA/total trials)* 100

Interval 1	A: 1	B: 2	Exact? NO
Interval 2	A: 3	B: 3	Exact? YES
Interval 3	A: 2	B: 3	Exact? NO

Exact count: 1/3 of intervals have an exact IOA= 1/3 *100= 33% IOA

4.   **Trail By Trial IOA**: The number of intervals in which the observers recorded the same occurrence or nonoccurrence of the behavior. Either recorded a response or did not record a response. The total data does not matter, only whether or not there was a response.

Formula: (Trials in agreement/trials total) * 100

Interval 1	A: 0 (no response)	B: 0 (no response)	Agree? YES
Interval 2	A: 1 (response)	B: 0 (no response)	Agree? NO
Interval 3	A: 1 (response)	B: 1 (response)	Agree? YES

Trail by trial IOA: 2 trials in agreement/3 trials total *100= 67%

Temporal/Duration IOA

1.   **Total Duration IOA**: percentage of agreement regarding the total duration
Formula: (shorter duration/longer duration)*100
It is the same as the total count IOA but with durations.

2.   **Mean Duration per Occurrence IOA**: record the duration for each occurrence, add up all the durations for all the behaviors, then divide by the total # of behaviors.
Formula: (Duration IOA Bx1+ Duration IOA Bx2+ ...) / Tot. # of Behaviors

Time Sampling Procedure IOA

1.   **Interval by Interval IOA**: Identify intervals with 100% IOA and divide by the total number of intervals.
Formula: (#of intervals in agreement/Tot. # of intervals) *100

2.   **Scored Interval IOA**: Identify intervals in which both observers scored an occurrence of the behavior in the interval. Then divide by the total number of intervals in which 1 or both observers recorded an occurrence.
Formula: (#of intervals both agreed there was an occurrence of behavior/Tot.#intervals at least 1 observer recorded an occurrence)*100

3.   **Unscored Interval IOA**: same as scored but for non-occurrence of behavior.
Formula: (#of intervals both agreed there was non-occurrence of behavior/Tot.#intervals at least 1 observer recorded non-occurrence)*100

C-9 Select A Measurement System To Obtain Representative Data Given The Dimensions Of Behavior And The Logistics Of Observing And Recording

When selecting a measurement method, consider:
- The behavior change goals
- Expected direction of behavior change
- The relative ease of detecting occurrences of behavior
- The environments, where and times when the behavior will be measured
- The availability and skills of personnel who will observe and record the behavior

Threats to Measurement Validity:
- Indirect measurement: measuring behavior in some way different from the behavior of interest.
- Measuring the wrong dimension: E.g., measuring rate when you should have measured duration.
- Measurement Artifacts: data give a misleading picture of the behavior because of the way measurement was conducted. For example, discontinuous measurement, limiting measurement scales (E.g., reporting client can only read 5 words after giving him only 5 words to read), or poorly scheduled observations (E.g., behavior occurs in the morning, data are collected in the afternoon).

Threats to Accuracy and Reliability:
- Human error: 1st threat
- Poorly designed measurement system: unnecessary steps or a complex system create a loss of accuracy and reliability. To reduce this, use a simple measurement system.
- Inadequate/poor observer training
- Observer drift: the unintended change in the way an observer collects data, a drift from the operational definition of the behavior of interest. To minimize this, collect IOA data and retrain observers on the correct operational definitions.
- Measurement bias: inaccurate measurement in which data over/underestimate the value of the event. It could be caused by the observer's expectations. The observer has expectations that the target behavior should occur at a certain level, under a particular condition in the environment. To avoid this, use naïve observers (observer that measures a target behavior but that is unaware of the study's purpose).
- Observer reactivity: measurement error caused by an observer's awareness that others are evaluating the data he reports and he is being monitored.

There are 2 types of errors that may be made in conducting ABA research:
- Type I error (False Positive): Assuming the IV affected the DV, when it actually did NOT do so.
- Type II error (False Negative): Assuming the IV did NOT affect the DV, when it actually did. Visual analysis used in ABA tends to lead to more type II errors.

C-10 Graph Data To Communicate Relevant Quantitative Relations (E.g., Equal-Interval Graphs, Bar Graphs, Cumulative Records)

Data is collected through measurement and it's the medium with which behavior analysts work.

Graphs are a relatively simple format for the visual display of relationships among and between measurements. The purpose of graphs is to:

1. Provide immediate access to an ongoing visual record of the participant's behavior

2. Explore interesting variations in behavior as they occur

3. Interpret the results of a study or treatment

4. Enable independent judgment and interpretations of the meaning and significance of behavior change

5. Effective sources of feedback to the people whose behavior they represent

6. Facilitate the communication, dissemination, and comprehension of behavior change among different recipients

There are different types of graphs: equal interval line graph, bar graph, cumulative records, scatterplot, and standard celeration chart.

Choose the graph that demonstrates the most ethical and valid representation of the target behavior.

Equal Interval Line Graph (AKA: Line Graph, Frequency Polygons)

Based on the Cartesian coordinate system, a line graph has both of its axes numbered with equal interval scales. It is the most common graph used in ABA. The line graph communicates data and its changes over time: level, trend, variability, range, and the number of data points.

Parts of the graph:

- Horizontal axis (AKA: X-axis, Abscissa): the passage of time, independent variable (IV)

- Vertical axis (Y-axis, Ordinate): dependent variable, dimension of behavior (DV). On this axis, you can see changes in the level, trend, and variability in the data.

- Origin: usually 0, the middle point where X and Y meet.

- Condition change line: major change, full line to indicate the introduction or withdrawal of intervention.

- Phase change line: minor change, dotted line.

- Condition label: description of the condition.

- Data points: a quantifiable measure of the target behavior recorded given the observation period, and the time under which the behavior occurred. If there are different data set, use different symbols for each set (we don't use colors on ABA graphs).

- Data path: a straight line connecting successive data points. The level and trend of behavior between successive data points are the primary focus for the interpretation and analysis of graphed data. Do not connect data points if there was a long break between sessions (E.g., vacation, illness), or for follow-up data.

- Figure caption: a concise statement that, in combination with the axis and its condition labels, provides the reader with sufficient information to identify the IV, the DV and explains the symbols used and unplanned events.

The y-axis should be shorter than the x-axis and maximum 4 data paths can be displayed on one graph.

Bar Graph (AKA: Histogram)

Data display that uses heights of bars to indicate the value of each variable. It is most effective in summarizing data sets when conditions or individuals are not related to each other or for group summative performance. It does not indicate any variability or trends in data. On the x-axis there is no successive time displayed.

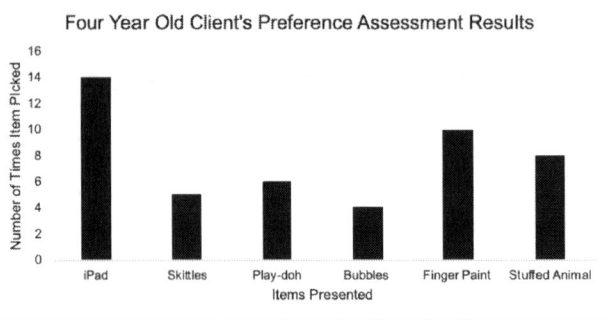

Cumulative Record

It was developed by B.F. Skinner. It's a line graph that shows the cumulative instances of behavior.

It is constructed by adding the number of responses recorded during each observation period to the total number of responses recorded during all previous observation periods.

Each data point indicates the total number of responses up to that point in time.

•   X-axis: the period of time

•   Y-axis: total number of behavior recorded since the start of the data collection. The steeper the slope, the higher the rate of responses. A flat horizontal line is no responses occurred during that period. (the line never decreases)

Use:

•   Desirable when a total number of responses over time is important, or when progress toward a specific goal can be measured in cumulative units of behavior (dollars accumulated, words learned, total hours of supervision)

•   Good source of feedback to the participant because it doesn't show decreasing trends (not aversive)

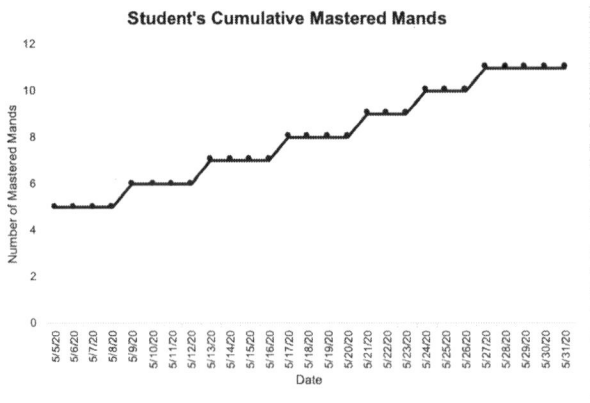

Standard Celeration Chart (AKA: Ratio Chart, Multiply-Divide Chart)

Developed by Ogden Lindsley in Precision Teaching, to analyze how the frequency of behavior changes over time. It is a standard ratio chart that can accommodate response rates as low as 1 per 24 hours or as high as 1000 per minute. There are four standard charts: a daily chart with 140 calendar days, a weekly chart, a monthly chart, and a yearly chart.

Used in charting academics, for social behaviors, in self-monitoring, and to increase fluency.

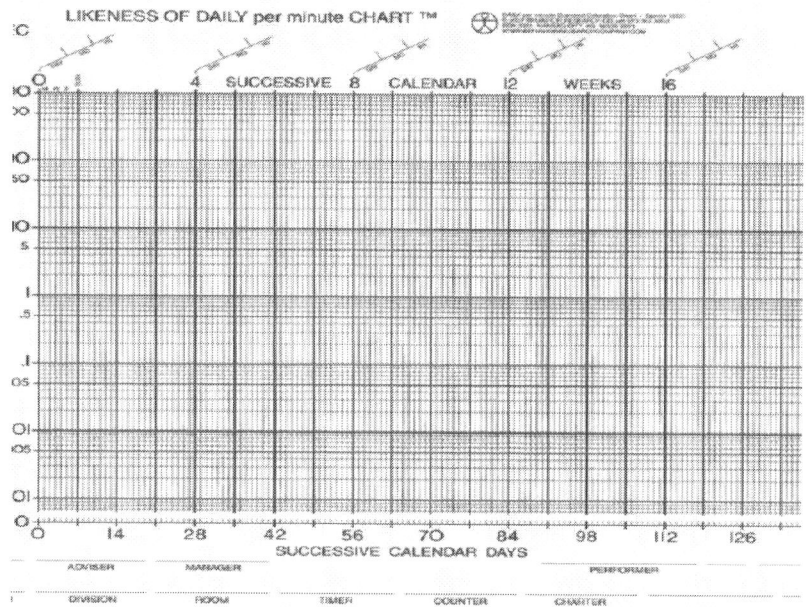

Scatterplot (AKA: Pattern Analysis)

A graphic display used to discover the temporal distribution of target behavior. It graphically shows whether the behavior's occurrence is typically associated with certain time periods.

On the y-axis, there is usually the time of day and on the x-axis the days.

Data points are not connected.

It only gives you a hypothesis of the function and replacement behaviors are not offered.

C-11 Interpret Graphed Data

Visual Analysis

The effects of treatment should be visually inspectable on a graph. We analyze how data points change in different conditions and phases of the treatment.

When examining the graphs we look at the level, the trend and the variability of the data.

Level

The level is the mean value of a set of data points, usually across an entire condition or phase. It's a horizontal line drawn at the average value of the set of data points that shows the degree of variability or stability of the behavior. A shift in level occurs when levels of data change between phases or conditions. This allows the practitioner to evaluate the effect of the change in the IV.

E.g., in the graph below, the baseline phase shows a low level of behavior while during the intervention phase the behavior occurs at high levels.

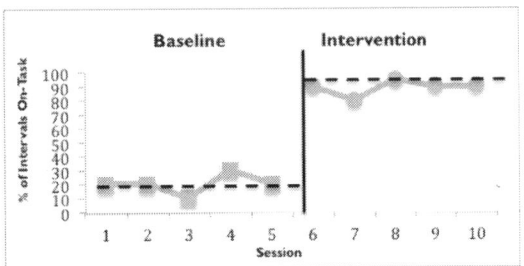
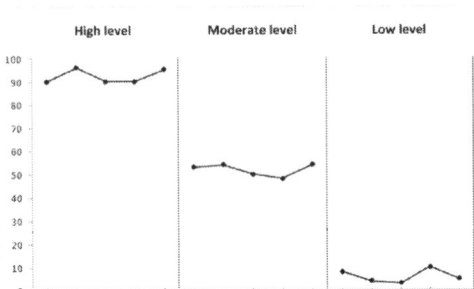

- Mean Level: Add all the data points and divide the sum by the total number of data points.

E.g. Data on the y-axis are 2,4,5. The mean is (2+4+5)/3=3.7

- Median Level: use when the client has extreme outliers. Put the data from the smallest to the largest and select the middle number as the median. If the number of data is even, calculate the average between the 2 middle data points.

E.g., Data on y-axis are 2,8,4. In order are 2,4,8. The median is 4.

Trend

The trend is a straight line that indicates the overall direction of the data path through a set of data points. The easiest way to draw a trend line is by hand. To help you, trend lines always have an equal number of data points above and below the line.

E.g., In the graph below, the baseline phase shows a decreasing trend as the data points are "going down." The intervention phase shows an increasing trend as the data points are "going up."

Finally, where it shows a "no trend", it's because the data are not going up or down.

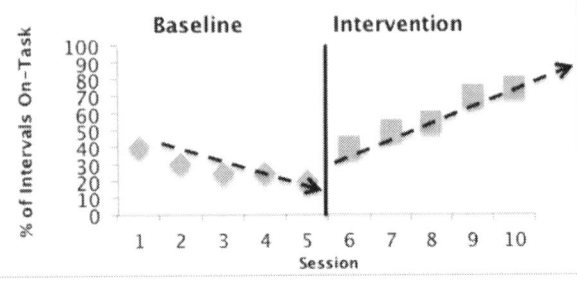
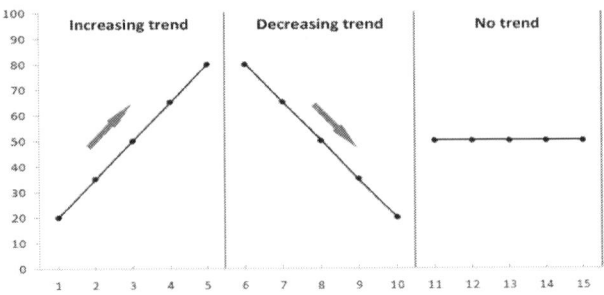

Variability

The variability of data is the extent to which measures of behavior under the same environmental conditions diverge from one another. It relates to how different the scores are from each other. Variability is the opposite of stability. The greater the variability, the greater the need for additional data. It also means you have low or no control over the elements that effect your client's behavior.

In the graph below, the baseline phase shows far more variability, so it's harder to predict where the next data point will fall. During the intervention phase, data are shown highly stable.

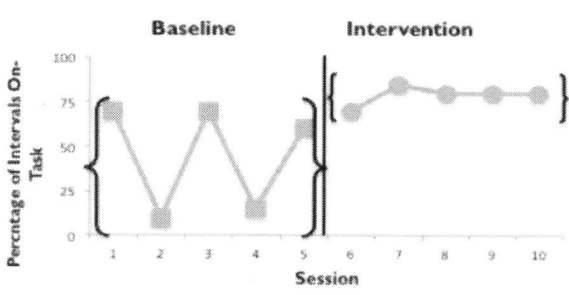

Coffee and Notes:

Shhh...

D.   Experimental Design

D-1:   Distinguish between dependent and independent variables.

D-2:   Distinguish between internal and external validity.

D-3:   Identify the defining features of single-subject experimental designs (e.g., individuals serve as their own controls, repeated measures, prediction, verification, replication).

D-4:   Describe the advantages of single-subject experimental designs compared to group designs.

D-5:   Use single-subject experimental designs (e.g., reversal, multiple baseline,multielement, changing criterion).

D-6:   Describe rationales for conducting comparative, component, and parametric analyses.

D-1 Distinguish Between Dependent And Independent Variables

We use 2 variables in experimentation:

Dependent Variable (Dv-Target Behavior)

It's the variable studied to see the effect of the IV in an experiment.

In applied behavior analysis, it represents some measure of a socially significant behavior (E.g., Rate, duration). It is the target behavior that we are measuring and that we want to change.

It is so labeled because we want to see if, in fact, it is dependent on the IV manipulated by the researcher.

In the graph, it is shown in the y-axis with different measures of the behavior.

E.g., rate of hitting, duration of tantrums, number of worksheets completed

Independent Variable (Iv- Intervention/Treatment)

It's the variable that the researcher systematically manipulates in an experiment to see whether changes in the IV produce reliable changes in the dependent variable.

Sometimes called the intervention or treatment variable.

It is usually an environmental event or condition that can be controlled by the researcher independently of the subject's behavior.

In the graph, it is shown in the x-axis as treatment during sessions/days/times.

E.g., extinction, different schedules of reinforcement, prompting, Time out procedure, token delivery.

The experimental design aims to demonstrate a functional relation between IV and DV and evaluate the interventions' effectiveness.

We say that we reached experimental control when systematic changes in the environment result in predictable and orderly changes in behavior.

D-2 Distinguish Between Internal And External Validity

There are two major types of validity:

Internal Validity

The extent to which changes in the behavior (DV) are due to the independent variable (IV) and not the result of uncontrolled or confounding variables.

If you have high internal validity, you have a high experimental control/functional relation because the intervention changes the behavior.

E.g., of good internal validity: the experimental design demonstrated that the token system reduced calling out and increased hand-raising with Jane. No other variables were involved.

Extraneous Variables: any aspect of the environment that must be held constant. It is usually something that the experimenter is aware of. E.g., light, room, temperature

Confounding Variables: uncontrolled factors, not expected by the experimenter and that can't be planned. E.g., earthquake

Threats To Internal Validity:

- Observer drift: the observer unknowingly changes the way a measurement system is applied
- Reactivity: changes in client behavior due to being observed.
- Observer bias/expectations: your expectations that data will change in a particular direction
- Attrition: participants drop out during the course of the study.
- Testing/Practice: responding improves for repeating the behavior.
- Maturation: changes in the client over the course of the study. (E.g., development of the client's verbal behavior. Looking at the data when he was 2yo compared to now that is 6yo)
- Adaptation: repeated presentation of a particular stimulus reduce the responses

External Validity

The degree to which a study's findings have generality to other subjects, settings, and/or behaviors.

Can your intervention be applied to other studies, other children, or other settings?

It relies on replication: intrasubject (same subject used) and intersubject (different subject used).

E.g., the token system reduced calling out and increased hand-raising also in a new classroom or with other children.

Internal validity is more important than external validity because generalization is irrelevant if the IV did not cause the change.

Two Main Errors In Research:

- Type 1- False Positive: assuming the IV effected the DV but it actually didn't
- Type 2- False Negative: assuming the IV didn't impact the DV but it did.

Social Validity

This refers to the applied dimension of behavior analysis. It is the extent to which target behaviors are appropriate, intervention procedures are acceptable, and important and socially significant changes in target behavior are produced. It answers the question, "did this make a difference?".

D-3 Identify The Defining Features Of Single-Subject Experimental Designs (E.g., Individuals Serve As Their Own Controls, Repeated Measures, Prediction, Verification, Replication)

Single-Subject Design (Aka Single-Case Design, Within Subject Design)

Most experiments in ABA are single-subject designs.

It is an experimental design where each participant serves as their own control, using repeated measures, a steady-state strategy for prediction and verification, and visual analysis of graphed data. It doesn't mean there is only 1 participant but can be more (4-8). Each participant is graphed separately.

Individuals Serve As Their Own Controls

It means comparing one individual's behavior to their own behavior in different conditions. Comparisons are made within an individual's behavior before and after the treatment.

Repeated Measures

It means collecting a lot of data on the DV, over an extended period of time and repeated observations.

Visual Analysis

Data are graphed, and we can examine changes in level, trend, or variability as a function of the change in the IV.

Steady-State Strategy (Aka Stable State Responding)

A pattern of responding that exhibits relatively little variation in its measured dimensional quantities over a period of time. The requirement is that behavior must reach a steady-state prior to making changes in the IV. This enables a form of inductive reasoning called Baseline logic (prediction, verification, replication).

- A stable baseline is the most desirable to the introduction of the IV.
- A descending or ascending baseline reveals that behavior is currently in the process of changing.
- A variable baseline means that there are uncontrolled environmental variables, do not introduce the IV but wait out until data are stable.

The logic behind single-subject designs is 1) Prediction, 2) Verification, and 3) Replication.

The baseline data predict behavior by affirming the consequent, it is the original data, the control condition of the study and what the treatment outcome is compared to.

Baseline data may sometimes include an already present IV.

Verification refers to demonstrating that the baseline response would have continued had no intervention been implemented.

Replication occurs when a previously observed behavior change is reproduced.

Prediction

It is defined as the anticipated outcome of a presently unknown or future measurement.

An explicit assumption can be made: If the independent variable were not applied, the baseline would remain the same and would not change.

Verification

It means verifying the original prediction of unchanging baseline measures.

It can be accomplished by demonstrating that the prior level of baseline responding would have remained unchanged had the independent variable not been introduced. If that is demonstrated, this operation reduces the probability that some uncontrolled variable was responsible for the observed change in behavior.

It helps to show that the IV has control of the behavior.

Replication

It means repeating independent variable manipulations conducted previously in the study and obtaining similar outcomes. It demonstrates the change either across multiple individuals or multiple times with the same individual.

It is necessary to evaluate internal validity but also to determine the generality of findings in other environments, subjects, or for different behaviors.

It demonstrates reliability and believability.

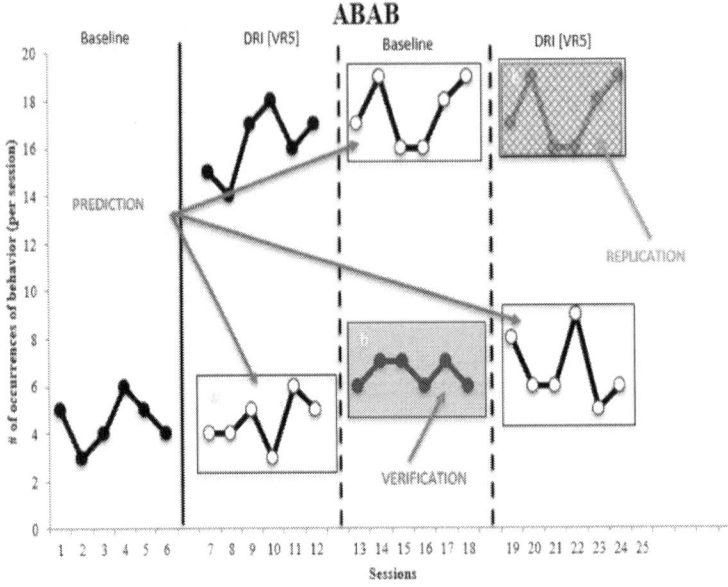

D-4 Describe The Advantages Of Single-Subject Experimental Designs Compared To Group Designs

	Single Case Design	Group Design
Control	Each individual as own control	Between groups
IV	Different conditions	1 condition
# Of Individuals	1 individual or few, many observations	Many people, few observations
Data Analysis	Graph/visual analysis and experimental control	Statistics and group average
IV Introduction	When DV stable	Randomized
Generalization	Replication	Random selection

Group Designs

Randomly select a poll of subjects from the relevant population, divide the subjects into experimental and control groups, apply the IV to the experimental group, and posttest. It is mostly used in psychology, sociology etc.

Single-Subject Design

Single-subject design is what behavior analysts use most. It helps to reveal information concerning individual participants while group designs seek to determine effectiveness on a population.

Single-case designs compare the dependent variable to previous data points, making the subject of the design their own control. Group designs compare the DV across participant groups.

Single-subject designs commonly use fewer subjects and take less time to run the conditions since there are fewer participants than in group design. In single-subject design, it is common for only one variable to be manipulated to ensure the change in behavior is a result of the IV, it also emphasizes the variations between individuals. Replication is a key feature of single-subject designs which helps to establish higher internal validity than group designs within the experiment.

D-5 Use Single-Subject Experimental Designs (E.g., Reversal, Multiple Baseline, Multielement, Changing Criterion)

Experimental Design	Multiple Baseline	Changing Criterion	Reversal	Multielement
IV-DV	1 IV 2+ DVs	1 IV 1 DV	1 IV 1 DV	2-4 IVs 1 DV
Use	Generalization	Acquisition targets, reducing challenging behaviors	Strongest proof of functional relation	Comparing most effective IV

Reversal Design (AKA: Withdrawal Design, BAB, ABAB Design)

It's an experimental design in which baseline and intervention alternate. The researcher attempts to verify the effect of the independent variable by "reversing" responding to a level obtained in a previous condition. There are at least 3 phases:

A- baseline phase in which the independent variable is absent

B- intervention phase where the independent variable is introduced

A- return to baseline conditions and withdrawal of the independent variable

B- (optional but preferred) reintroduce IV and continue to collect data until stability

Experimental control is demonstrated if behavior changes systematically as a function of the introduction and withdrawal of the IV.

Irreversibility: not appropriate in evaluating the effect of a treatment variable that, by its very nature, cannot be withdrawn once it has been presented.

E.g., after participating in a workshop you cannot unlearn what you heard. The exposure provided by that experience could not be withdrawn.

Ethical concern: for Self-injurious or dangerous behaviors it may be determined that withdrawing an intervention associated with improvement for even a few one-session probes would be unethical. Use BAB design.

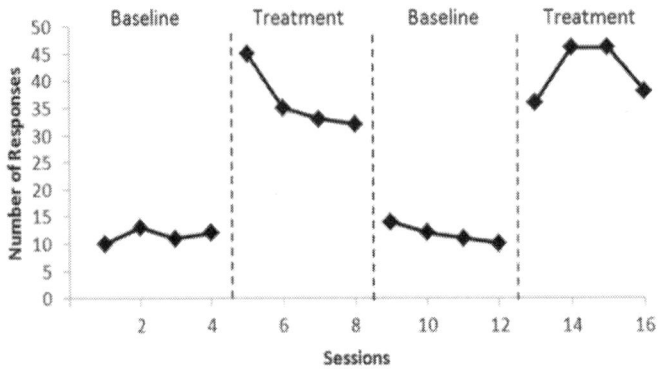

Repeated Reversal (ABABABAB)

When you prolong the ABAB design. Stronger evidence of control.

B-A-B Reversal Design

This is a variation of the A-B-A design and in this version the intervention is introduced immediately without a baseline. This happens when the target behavior is dangerous and allowing the behavior to occur during baseline could result in harm to the subject. In this variation, intervention (B) is immediately implemented and may or may not be removed until the dangerous behavior is completely extinguished or reduced to safe levels. Weaker than ABA design because it doesn't allow for a comparison of IV effects on baseline.

Multiple Treatment Reversal Design (2+ IV, 1 DV)

This is a variation of the A-B-A design that includes more than one intervention being reversed. In this design, there is a baseline (A), intervention 1 (B), and intervention 2 (C). This would look like ABCACB or ABACABAC or other sequences. For example, you may want to test a response cost and a time-out procedure and would conduct reversals to demonstrate experimental control.

Be careful to Sequence effects (AKA: Carryover effects): the order of the conditions influences the changes in the DV. You should randomize the treatment sequence to avoid this.

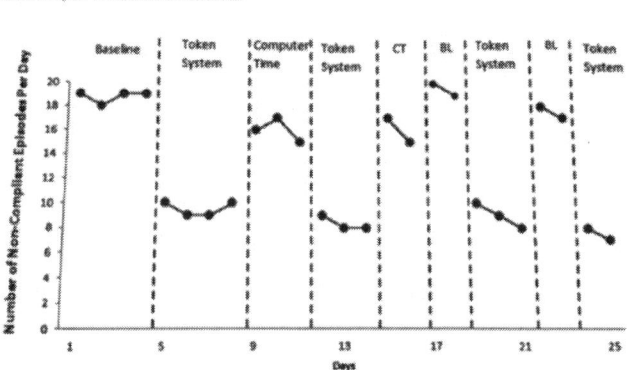

Noncontingent Reinforcement (NCR) Reversal Design

This is a variation of the reversal design. It is used to examine the effects of NCR and contingent reinforcement. It starts with baseline and then alternates NCR and contingent SR phases.

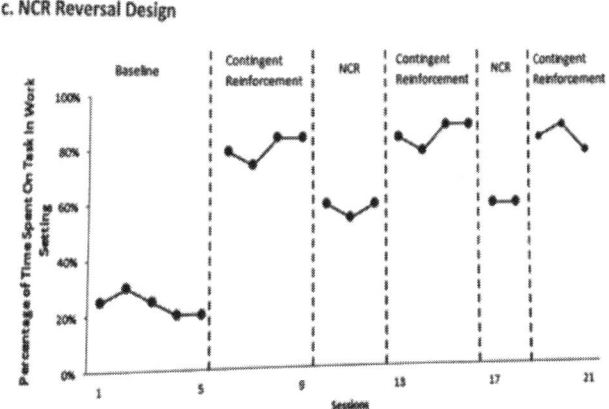

DRO/DRA/DRI Reversal Design

This is a variation of the reversal design. It is used to examine the effects of SR by using DRO/DRA/DRI as a control condition.

Multielement Design (Aka: Alternating Treatment Design, Simultaneous Treatment Design, Concurrent Schedules Design). 2+Iv, 1 Dv

It's an experimental design in which there is a rapid alternation of two or more independent variables while their effects on the target behavior (DV) are measured. Each condition is associated with a distinct stimulus (SD).

A functional relationship is demonstrated between the treatment and behavior when different treatments consistently correspond to different levels of behavior.

We look for a condition in which behavior is different relative to other conditions, this means that one data paths show little or no overlap with the other data paths and so it is higher or lower.

Advantages:

- Participants can receive treatments immediately
- It evaluates several treatment conditions at the same time and shows which IV is best
- It does not require steady-state responding before introducing new conditions. (vs reversal)
- No withdrawal of the treatment is required
- Use for highly variable behavior

Considerations:

- Multiple treatment inferences: the confounding effects of one treatment on a subject's behavior being influenced by the effects of another treatment administered in the same study
- Sequence effect
- Limited capacity (max of 4 conditions)
- Some treatments are only effective after a certain period of time
- Do not use if the individual has difficulty with discriminations
- Only for reversible behavior

E.g., in the graph below you can observe the shaping procedure being more effective compared to the DRA intervention.

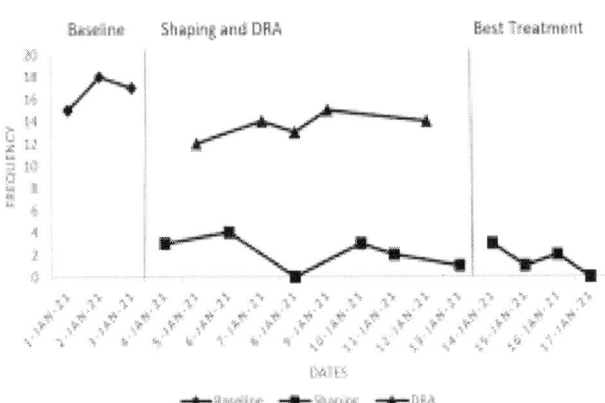

Variations:

- Multielement with baseline: stability is needed in baseline before implementing the treatments.
- Multielement with baseline and final best treatment phase or final participant's choice

Multiple Baseline Design (1 IV and 2 or more DVs)

Experimental design in which two or more independent baselines are established and the independent variable is evaluated through the staggered introduction on each baseline.

It's essentially a multiple A-B design.

Allow practitioners to analyze the effects of an independent variable across multiple

behaviors, participants, or settings without having to withdraw the treatment variable to verify that the improvements in behavior are a direct result of the application of the

treatment.

Verification is established when you add a baseline, and replication is established when

the results are replicated with another individual/setting/or behavior.

3 to 5 tiers are the most common and the introduction of the IV is always done after a stable baseline.

Considerations:

- Requires a lot of time
- Only appropriate for behaviors that are independent from each other
- Long baseline phase
- It shows generalization
- Use for behaviors that are irreversible or when it's not appropriate to remove an effective IV.

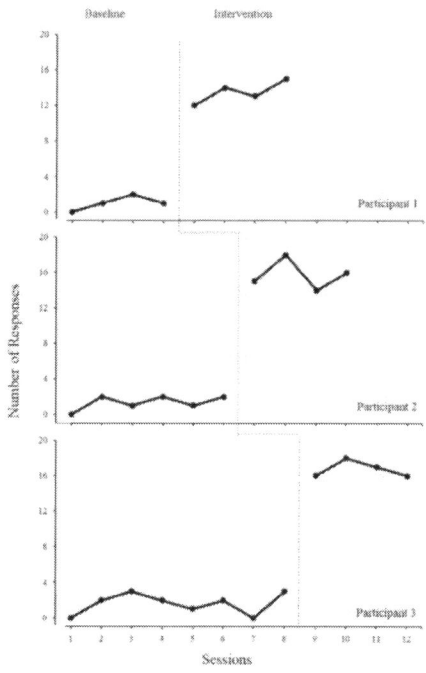

Variations:

- across subjects: different individuals with the same DV (behavior) in the same setting, and same IV (treatment) introduced.

E.g., Used DRA procedure with 3 different clients (Jane, Jennifer, and Joy) to reduce aggression (DV) in the classroom.

- across settings: 1 individual with the same DV but in different settings, with the same IV.

E.g., Used DRA procedure with the same client to reduce aggression (DV) in the classroom, at home, and at the gym.

- across behaviors: 1 individual with different DVs (behaviors), same IV introduced.

E.g., Used DRA procedure with the same client to reduce aggression (DV1), non-compliance (DV 2), and disruption (DV 3).

Multiple Probe Design
It's a variation of the multiple baseline design that uses intermittent measures, or probes, of behavior during baseline.

Data are not collected for every session/day because continuous measurement is not possible, impractical or too costly.

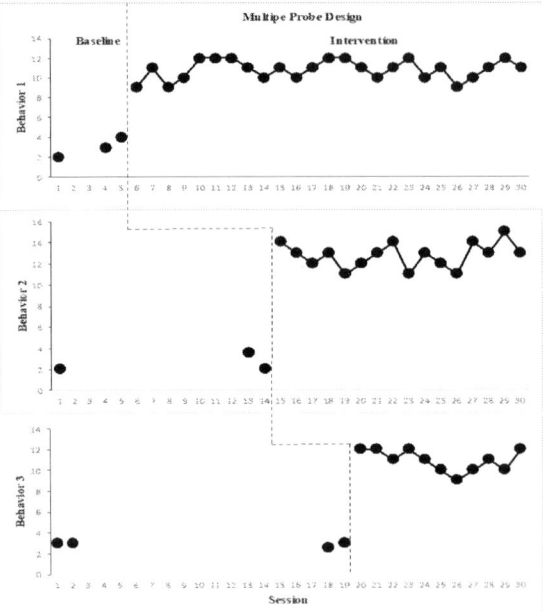

Non-Concurrent Multiple Baseline Across Subjects
Nonconcurrent multiple baseline designs stagger the timing of baseline-to-intervention changes across various entities, but the baselines and intervention phases are not contemporaneous across each of the tiers. Although considered less rigorous than concurrent multiple baseline designs, nonconcurrent designs have a degree of flexibility that may allow for their use in studying complex social contexts.

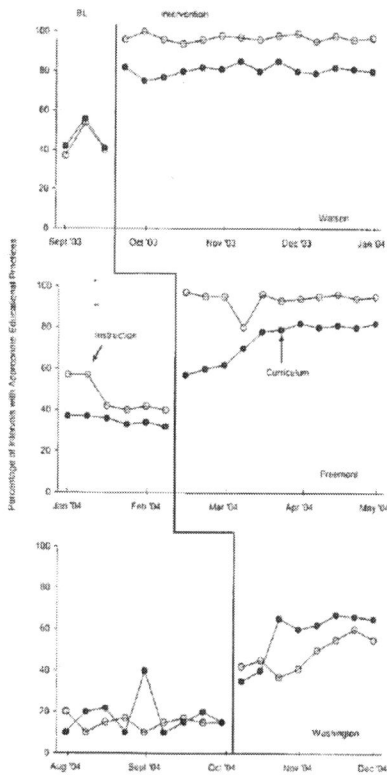

Delayed Multiple Baseline Design

It's a variation of the multiple baseline design where the initial baseline and intervention begin and subsequent baselines are added in a delayed fashion. The data collection for the baseline doesn't start for all the tiers at the same time.

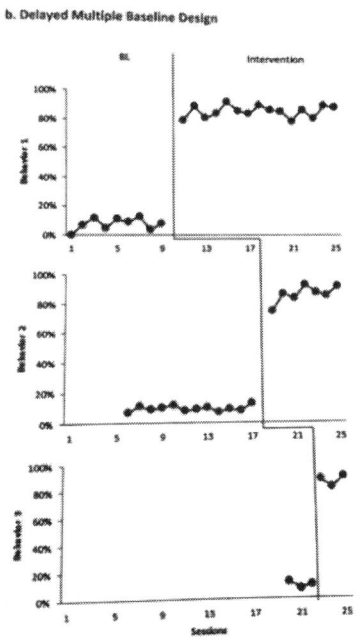

b. Delayed Multiple Baseline Design

Changing Criterion Design (1 IV and 1 DV)

Experimental design in which an initial baseline phase is followed by a treatment phase divided into stepwise sub-phases, each with a different behavioral criterion.

•   Baseline on a single behavior

•   Treatment phases: each phase is associated with a performance criterion that is either increased or decreased across subsequent phases.

Each sub-phase is compared to the previous one (that serves as a baseline) and once you reach the criteria you move on to the next criteria in the next phase.

E.g., Decreasing gradually the number of cigarettes smoked per day. Baseline: 15 cigarettes per day. 1st goal is to reduce to 12/day, then 10/day, then 7, and so on...

Note: In the changing criterion design behaviors are already in the client's repertoire. We are just increasing or decreasing a dimension of that known behavior.

For this reason, this design can't be used for shaping (used for novel behavior) where we are reinforcing successive approximations towards the terminal behavior.

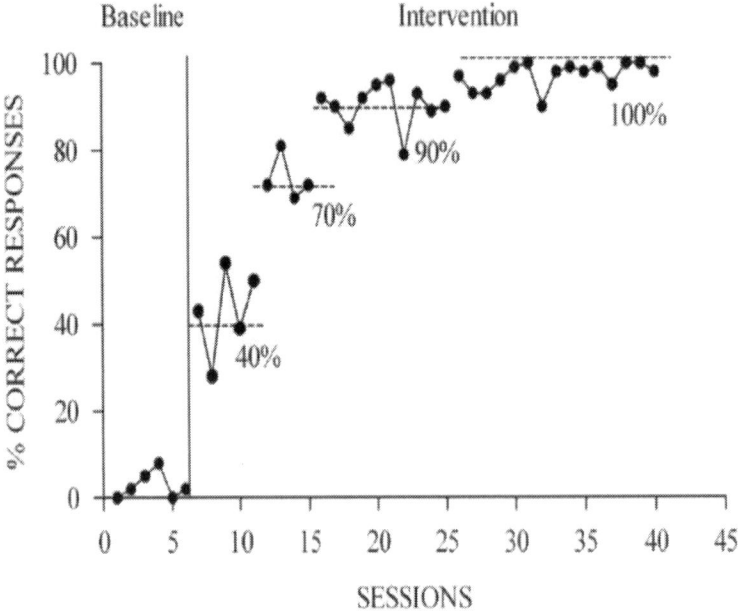

D-6 Describe Rationales For Conducting Comparative, Component, And Parametric Analyses

Non Parametric Analysis

Present and remove the IV to evaluate the effect on your client's DV. On/Off procedure.

E.g., the medication is given or not given to the client.

Parametric Analysis

Does more or less of the intervention work better? How much IV?

Purpose: evaluate the effects of various ranges of an intervention (IV).

E.g., to evaluate the range of values for time out that is most effective, you would conduct a parametric analysis using 1 minute, 5 minutes, 10 minutes, and so on.

Note: No absence/presence of the IV like in nonparametric analysis but changing in values of the IV.

Component Analysis (AKA Composite Analysis)

How effective is the intervention when various components are added or subtracted in a treatment package?

Purpose: determine which part of an independent variable is responsible for behavior change.

It can be done by systematically withdrawing treatment components from a multipart intervention to identify the effective elements of a treatment package.

E.g., FCT, DRO, VR5. Add (or take out) one component at a time to see which component or combo of treatments is most effective.

Comparative Analysis

Does one intervention work better than another?

This is a research design that involves comparing two or more independent variables in a multielement design.

Typically, the relative effectiveness of two different interventions is measured on a single dependent variable.

E.g., comparing the effects of NCR vs. DRO procedure with a client.

Coffee and Notes:

Shhh...

Section 2: Applications

E   **Ethics**

F   **Behavior Assessment**

G   **Behavior Change Procedures**

H   **Selecting and Implementing Interventions**

I   **Personnel Supervision and Management**

GRAPH.

ANALYZE.

Repeat.

Change the world!

E.   **Ethics**

 **WARNING**

This section is just a SUMMARY of the BCBA Code, and it does NOT include all the info necessary for you to know and understand as a behavior analyst. It is HIGHLY recommended to read carefully the most current version of the Code and all the documents available at

https://bacb.com/wp-content/ethics-code-for-behavior-analysts/

E-1 Introduction

Ethics refers to the behaviors, practices, and decisions that address three basic questions:
What is the right thing to do? What is worth doing? What does it mean to be a good behavior analyst?

We need to consider:
- Personal histories that could influence the practitioner's behavior.

The analyst's training and experiences will balance negative biases and predispositions that may carry over their personal or cultural background.

To avoid this, they can seek help from supervisors or colleagues, review the research literature, consult case studies to determine past courses of successful actions, or excuse themselves from the case.
- The practice context: People work in homes, schools, community settings, and more. Consider ethical and legal concerns because something may be legal but unethical.
- Ethical codes of behavior: All professional organizations have generated or adopted ethical codes of behavior. These codes provide guidelines for association members to consider when deciding on a course of action or conducting their professional duties.
- Social validity: plan acceptable goals for the behavior change intervention and determine the best treatment.
- Cost-benefit ratio: balance between planning, implementing, and evaluating a treatment or intervention (the cost side) and projecting future potential gain by the person.
- Existing needs: Some behaviors are too severe and must be addressed quickly.
- Follow the professional code of conduct: the Golden rule is "do not do to others as you would have them do unto you."
- Self-regulate: the ethical practitioner seeks ways to calibrate decisions over time to ensure that values, contingencies, and rights and responsibilities are integrated.

Ethics is important because:
- Produce meaningful behavior change of social significance for the persons enthused by their care
- Reduce or eliminate harm (poor treatments, self-injury)
- Conform to the ethical standards of learned societies and professional organizations

The Code provides ethical rules for certified individuals. It is an enforceable document, and it is divided into 4 core Principles:

1.   Benefit others: This aspect of the code focuses on producing meaningful and socially significant change for the individuals we work with while doing no harm.
2.   Treating others with compassion, dignity, and respect: This aspect focuses on using an equitable approach to your clinical practice and respecting the client as a person, a unique individual, and a valued member of society. This also ensures that confidentiality is maintained and is a top priority.
3.   Behave with integrity: This aspect focuses on the truthfulness of the individual delivering a behavior service and that they are using professional judgment in making sound decisions based on their education, experience, and expertise.
4.   Ensure their competence: This aspect focuses on behavior analysts staying within their scope of practice and ensuring that they uphold their credentials.

Informed by the core principles, the ethics standards are organized into six sections:

1) Responsibility as a Professional
2) Responsibility in Practice
3) Responsibility to Clients and Stakeholders
4) Responsibility to Supervisees and Trainees
5) Responsibility in Public Statements
6) Responsibility in Research

Behavior Analysts

It refers to an individual who holds BCBA or BCaBA certification or an individual who has submitted a complete application for the BCBA or BCaBA.

Behavior Analytic Services

Those are services explicitly based on the principles and procedure of behavior analysis and are designed to change behavior in socially important ways. Ex: treatment, assessment, training, consultation, managing and supervising others, delivering continuing education, etc.

Client

Any beneficiary of the professional services provided by a behavior analyst. It includes:
• 	the direct recipient of services
• 	the parent, relative legal representative, or guardian of the recipient of services
• 	the employer, agency representative, or a third-party contractor for the services of the behavior analyst.
It does not include third-party insurers or payers.

Stakeholder

An individual, other than the client, who is impacted by and invested in the behavior analyst's service.

Supervisee

A person whose behavioral service delivery is overseen by a behavior analyst.

Trainee

Individual accruing fieldwork experience hours to fulfill the requirements for the BCaBA or the BCBA.

E-2 Responsibility As A Professional

1.01   Being Truthful

Behavior analysts are truthful and they promote truthful behavior in others. No illegal/fraudulent behavior. Give truthful info and correct if inaccurate information is provided.

1.02   Conforming with Legal and Professional Requirements

Follow the law and requirements of our professional community. Know the Code and be familiar with your state's licensing code of ethics.

1.03 Accountability

Be accountable for your actions and follow through on work commitments. If errors, take action in the best interest of the client and relevant parties.

1.04 Practicing within a Defined Role

Define and document your professional role in writing to all the relevant parties.

1.05 Practicing within Scope of Competence

Practice only within your scope of competence (professional activities that you can consistently perform with proficiency). If it's outside your scope but you want to work in new areas (e.g., new population, new procedures), you must do training, supervised experience, consultation, and/or co-treatment with a mentor. Otherwise, you need to refer/transition the client to another competent professional.

E.g., if you always worked with children with autism and your new client is an adult with developmental disabilities, you need to receive training, supervision and consult with a mentor or transition the case to someone more expert in that area.

1.06 Maintaining Competence

Actively engage in activities to maintain your knowledge and stay current with what is new in the field. Stay informed by reading relevant literature, attending conferences, participating in workshops and other training opportunities, receiving coaching, consultation, and mentorship, and maintaining professional credentials (CEUs: Continuing Education Units).

Continuing Education Requirements:
*   BCBA/BCBA-D: 32 CEs per 2 years Recertification cycle with 4hrs in Ethics
*   BCaBA: 20 CEs per 2 years Recertification cycle with 4hrs in Ethics

1.07 Cultural Responsiveness and Diversity

Engage in professional development activities to acquire knowledge and skills related to cultural responsiveness and diversity.

Evaluate your own biases and ability to address the needs of individuals with diverse needs and backgrounds. Evaluate these things also for your supervisees and trainees.

1.08 Nondiscrimination

Do not discriminate against others. Behave in an equitable and inclusive manner regardless of sex, age, gender, race, disability, relationship status, ethnicity, immigration status, national origin, religion, sexual orientation, socioeconomic status, etc.

1.09 Nonharassment
Do not engage in behavior that is harassing or hostile towards others.

1.10 Awareness of Personal Biases and Challenges
Ensure that professional work is not compromised by personal biases or challenges (mental/physical health conditions, financial/legal/relationship challenges, etc). If so, take appropriate steps to resolve the issues and document all actions taken.

1.11 Multiple Relationships (AKA: Dual relationship)
Avoid creating multiple relationships with clients or colleagues. A dual relationship occurs when you acquire 2 or more roles, professional and personal, with the client, stakeholder or supervisee.
E.g., You start dating the father of your client. (no!)
E.g., You provide ABA therapy to your cousin that has autism (no!)
Communicate the risks of multiple relationships and continue to monitor and take immediate actions to solve them in case they arise. Document all actions taken.

1.12 Giving and Receiving Gifts
Do not give gifts to or accept gifts from clients, stakeholders, or supervisees with a value of more than $10 US dollars.
Make it clear at the beginning of the professional relationship and send policy reminders (for example, before Christmas).
It is considered a violation of the code if the gifts are regularly expected and frequent(e.g., a gift for meeting every goal with the client).
A gift is acceptable if it is a form of gratitude, infrequent and it doesn't result in a financial benefit to the recipient.

1.13 Coercive and Exploitative Relationships
Do not abuse your power or authority by coercing or exploiting persons you have authority over. (trainees, supervisees)

1.14 Romantic and Sexual Relationships
Do not have a romantic relationship with:
- Current clients, stakeholders, or trainees: Never! It could cause a conflict of interests and impaired judgment.
- Former clients: a minimum of 2 years from the date the professional relationship ended.
- Former supervisee/trainees: until you document that the professional relationship has ended
Do not provide supervision to a previous romantic partner unless the relationship ended at least 6 months ago.

1.15 Responding to Requests
Make appropriate efforts to respond to requests for information and comply with the deadlines of relevant individuals.
E.g., If a family requests your BCBA certificate, show it to them.

1.16 Self-Reporting Critical Information
Report to all relevant entities (e.g., BCBA) any critical information (e.g., DUI).

E-3 Responsibility In Practice

2.01 Providing Effective Treatment

Prioritize clients' rights and needs in service delivery. Provide services that are based on scientific evidence and principles of ABA (Conceptually Systematic).

The evidence-based best practice relies on scientific literature for treatment choices and data-driven decisions when assessing the effectiveness of treatment. Do no harm.

Implement nonbehavioral services only if you have the required education, training, and credentials.

2.02 Timeliness

Deliver services and service-related administrative responsibilities in a timely manner and on time. E.g., file your reports on time.

2.03 Protecting Confidential Information

Prevent the accidental sharing of information, and protect the confidentiality of clients/families/supervisees. Use specific forms to report breaches in confidentiality.

2.04 Disclosing Confidential Information

Share confidential information only when

- Informed consent is obtained
- Attempting to protect the client from harm to others, to self, or child abuse
- Resolving contractual or payment issues
- Preventing a crime or immediate crisis
- Compelled by court orders.

Even in those cases, only share info critical to the purpose of the communication.

2.05 Documentation Protection and Retention

Follow requirements for storing, transporting, and destroying documentation related to your professional activities. If you leave the company, the organization is responsible.

Know HIPAA laws and the laws of your state. Client records may need to be kept for 1-7 years.

HIPAA (Health Insurance Portability And Accountability Act): establishes rules about the transition/storing of client Protected Health Info and the client's privacy rights.

2.06 Accuracy in Service Billing and Reporting

Identify services accurately and include all required info on reports, bills, invoices, etc.

Do not bill nonbehavioral services under the authorization for behavioral services.

If inaccuracies in billing are discovered report, correct, and document all actions taken in a timely manner.

2.07 Fees

Communicate fees upfront and take steps to resolve any inaccuracy or conflict.

2.08 Communicating About Services

Use clear and understandable language. Describe the scope of services and the conditions under which the service will end. Explain the interventions before implementing them and share results when available. Provide the current set of credentials upon request.

2.09 Involving Clients and Stakeholders
Involve client and their families throughout the entire service relationship. They should help to identify the ultimate goals and meaningful outcomes based on their necessities and satisfactions.

2.10 Collaborating with Colleagues
Collaborate with colleagues from our own and other professions. Address conflicts if they arise, always in the client's best interest.
We mainly collaborate with speech therapists, occupational therapists, school staff, doctors, etc.

2.11 Obtaining Informed Consent
Informed Consent is the permission given by an individual with the legal right to consent before participating in services or research, or allowing their info to be used or shared.
Explain, obtain, reobtain, and document required informed consent.
3 required elements to ensure informed consent:
•   Capacity: the client has the capacity to make an informed decision. The client can rationally understand the procedures, risks, and relevant information. If mentally incapacitated, a legally authorized representative provides consent on behalf of the client.
•   Voluntary: the client's decision must be given in the absence of coercion or influence. And the decision can be withdrawn at any time.
•   Knowledge: the client have knowledge of all salient aspects of the procedure, risk, and benefits, and alternative procedures. The client is informed of his right to refuse treatment at any time.
Obtain Assent from clients when applicable.
Consent= legally, only a person over 18 years of age
Assent= agreement of children or anyone not able to give legal consent

2.12 Considering Medical Needs
Rule out medical needs before implementing any behavioral intervention.
Document referrals made to a medical professional and follow up after.

2.13 Selecting, Designing, and Implementing Assessments
Select assessments that are conceptually consistent with behavioral principles, based on scientific evidence, that meet diverse needs, focus on maximizing benefits, and minimize risks of harm to the client. Summarizes the procedures and results in writing.

2.14 Selecting, Designing, and Implementing Behavior-Change Interventions
Select interventions that are conceptually consistent with behavioral principles, based on scientific evidence and on assessment results, that meet diverse needs, prioritize positive SR procedures, maximize benefits, and minimize risks of harm to the client.
Summarize the behavior plan in writing.

2.15 Minimizing Risk of Behavior-Change Interventions
Select interventions that minimize harm to the client and stakeholders.
Recommend punishment or restrictive procedures only if anything else less intrusive didn't produce the desired results.
Conduct a Risk-Benefit analysis to evaluate the potential risks and benefits associated with a given intervention.

Continually evaluate and modify or discontinue the intervention promptly if it is ineffective.

2.16 Describing Behavior-Change Interventions Before Implementation
Before implementation describe in writing the objectives and procedures of the intervention, the projected time-lines, and the schedule of ongoing review.
For the success of the intervention consider if:
- The client is in agreement with the implementation of the procedure
- There are safety issues
- All the resources needed for the procedure are available
- There are SRs you can control to help implement the procedure.

2.17 Collecting and Using Data
Data is collected on target behaviors. Graphically display, summarize and make decisions based on the data. (Empiricism)

2.18 Continual Evaluation of the Behavior-Change Intervention
Monitoring and evaluating interventions are ongoing. If you are concerned that the intervention used by another professional is negatively impacting the client, review and address the issue with the other professional.

2.19 Addressing Conditions Interfering with Service Delivery
Identify environmental conditions that may interfere or prevent service delivery (e.g., frequent cancellations, not following the procedure). Remove or minimize those conditions, and document all actions taken with eventual outcomes.

E-4 Responsibility To Clients And Stakeholders

3.01 Responsibility to Clients
Act in the best interest of the client, do no harm, maximize benefits and minimize risks.
You are a mandated reporter so if you see something, say something. Don't report if it's secondhand evidence.

3.02 Identifying Stakeholders
Identifying stakeholders when providing services. If there are multiple stakeholders, identify relative obligations, document and communicate them at the beginning of the professional relationship to each stakeholder.

3.03 Accepting Clients
Only accept clients that are within your scope of competence and available resources.
Take appropriate steps to discuss and resolve any concerns and document all actions taken.
Ask yourself if ABA will change the behavior or if another therapy will be ideal for the client.

3.04 Service Agreement
Ensure there is a signed service agreement with the client and stakeholders outlining the responsibilities of all parties, the scope of the services provided, the behavior analyst's obligation under the code, and the procedure for submitting complaints to relevant parties. Update service agreements as needed.

3.05 Financial Agreements
Before beginning services, document agreed-upon compensation and billing practices with your clients and or funders. When funding circumstances change revisit the documentation.
Pro bono/free services are only provided under a specific service agreement and in compliance with the Code.

3.06 Consulting with Other Providers
Arrange for appropriate consultation with and referrals to other providers in the best interest of your clients. Inform the clients of the referral process and of the other provider's qualifications, then provide the client with 2/3 referral choices.

3.07 Third-Party Contracts for Services
Third-party is any individual or group other than the direct recipient of services who request and fund services on behalf of the client. Some examples include the school district, mental health agencies, and governmental entities. When behavior analysts enter into a signed contract to provide services to a client at the request of a 3rd party/ funding source they clarify the nature of the relationship with each party and ensure all of the contract responsibilities and obligations are identified.

3.08 Responsibility to the Client with Third-Party Contracts for Services
The client's welfare is above everything.
If the 3rd party requests services from you that are incompatible with your recommendations or outside of your scope of confidence, or that could result in a multiple relationship, resolve such conflicts in the best interest of the client.
If the conflict can't be resolved, obtain training or, refer to another behavior analyst or discontinue services.

3.09 Communicating with Stakeholders About Third-Party Contracted Services

Ensure that the parent or legally authorized representative is informed of the scope of services to be provided. They have the right to receive copies of all service documentation and data.

3.10 Limitations of Confidentiality
At the outset of the professional relationship, inform clients and stakeholders of the limitations of confidentiality and when info disclosures are required.

3.11 Documenting Professional Activity
Create and maintain detailed and high-quality documentation of every activity provided to ensure accountability. Think of the Technological dimension of ABA that makes our work replicable and communication or transition of services easier and faster.

3.12 Advocating for Appropriate Services
Advocate for evidence-based assessments and behavior change procedures.
Advocate for the appropriate amount and level of behavioral service provision and oversight required to meet defined client goals.

3.13 Referrals
Make referrals based on the needs of the clients and stakeholders and include multiple providers when available (2/3 referrals are ideal).
Disclose any relationship we have with the potential providers and any fees or incentives we may receive for the referrals. Document all actions and follow up with the client.

3.14 Facilitating Continuity of Services
Make efforts to facilitate the continuation of behavioral services in the vent of planned (leave of absence, relocation) or unplanned interruptions (illness, emergencies). When a service interruption occurs communicate to all the relevant parties the steps being taken and document all actions.

3.15 Appropriately Discontinuing Services
Services are discontinued when:
- All goals are met
- The client is not benefiting from the service
- The behavior analyst or supervisees are exposed to potentially harmful conditions that cannot be resolved
- The client requested discontinuation
- The stakeholders are not complying with the interventions despite appropriate efforts to address barriers.
- Services are no longer funded.

Provide a written plan for discontinuing services and document all actions taken.

3.16 Appropriately Transitioning Services
Include the service agreement the circumstances for transitioning the client to another behavior analyst within or outside of your organization.
Make appropriate efforts to manage transitions and minimize disruptions to services.
Provide a written plan that includes dates transitions activities and responsible parties and review the plan throughout the transition.

E-5 Responsibility To Supervisees and Trainees

4.01 Compliance with Supervision Requirements
The supervisee is any individual whose behavioral service delivery is overseen by a behavior analyst within the context of a defined relationship. Supervisees may include RBTs, BCBAs, BCaBAs. Behavior analysts have to comply to supervisor's requirements: 8hrs of supervisor training a curriculum outline and 3 hours of CEs in supervision for each certification cycle.

4.02 Supervisory Competence
Supervise and train others only within your scope of competence.

4.03 Supervisory Volume
Take on only the number of supervisees/volume of trainees that allows you to provide effective supervision and training.

4.04 Accountability in Supervision
Behavior analysts are accountable for supervisory practices and for the professional activities of supervisees and trainees.

4.05 Maintaining Supervision Documentation
Create, update, store, and dispose of documentation related to the supervisees or trainees by following all applicable requirements. Ensure that the documentation is accurate and complete. Retain supervision documentation for at least 7 years.

4.06 Providing Supervision and Training
Design and deliver supervision and training procedures that are evidence-based, focus on positive reinforcement, and are individualized for each supervisee.

4.07 Incorporating and Addressing Diversity
During supervision actively incorporate and address topics related to diversity.

4.08 Performance Monitoring and Feedback
Collect data on the performance of supervisees and provide formal and informal feedback designed to improve performance.
When performance problems arise develop, communicate, implement and evaluate an improvement plan to address the problem.

4.09 Delegation of Tasks
Delegate tasks to supervisees only after confirming that they can competently perform the task. Observe supervisees performing skills in order to provide training and feedback.

4.10 Evaluating Effects of Supervision and Training
Evaluate your own supervisory practices using feedback from others and client and supervisee outcomes. The evaluation is ongoing.

4.11 Facilitating Continuity of Supervision

Minimize interruption or disruption of supervision and make efforts to facilitate the continuation of supervision in the event of planned or unplanned interruptions.

4.12 Appropriately Terminating Supervision

If, for any reason, supervision needs to be terminated, develop a plan that minimizes negative impacts to the supervisee. Document all actions taken and eventual outcomes.

E-6 Responsibility In Public Statements

5.01 Protecting the Rights of Clients, Stakeholders, Supervisees, and Trainees
Protect the rights of clients, stakeholders, supervisees, and trainees in all public statements.
Public statements are the delivery of info in a public forum for the purpose of better informing that audience or providing a call to action.

5.02 Confidentiality in Public Statements
Protect the confidentiality of clients, supervisees, and trainees, except when allowed and make efforts to prevent accidental sharing of confidential or identifying information.

5.03 Public Statements by Behavior Analysts
Ensure that the public statements are truthful, do not mislead or exaggerate, and are based on existing research and behavioral conceptualization.
Do not provide specific advice related to a client's needs in public forums.

5.04 Public Statements by Others
Behavior analysts are responsible for public statements that promote professional activities regardless of who creates or publishes the statement.
Make effort to prevent others from making deceptive statements concerning their professional activities. In case of misleading statements, correct them and document all actions taken.

5.05 Use of Intellectual Property
Behavior analysts comply with intellectual property laws and obtain permission to use materials that have been trademarked or copyrighted. To appropriately use such materials they provide citations, attributions, trademark or copyright symbols.

5.06 Advertising Nonbehavioral Services
Do not advertise non-behavioral services as behavioral services. If behavior analysts provide non-behavioral services, they must be clearly distinguished from your behavioral services with a disclaimer.

5.07 Soliciting Testimonials from Current Clients for Advertising
Testimonial is any solicited or unsolicited recommendation from a client, stakeholder, or supervisee affirming the benefits received from a behavior analyst service.
Do not solicit testimonials from current clients.
That does not include unsolicited reviews on websites where the behavior analyst has no control over the content, but such content cannot be shared or used.

5.08 Using Testimonials from Former Clients for Advertising
Testimonials from former clients must be identified as solicited or unsolicited and include an accurate statement of the relationship between the behavior analyst and the testimonial.
Always consider the possibility that former clients may re-enter services.
If the testimonial is solicited provide a description of where and how the testimonial will appear, and that the testimonial can be withdrawn at any time.

5.09 Using Testimonials for Nonadvertising Purposes
Behavior analysts may use testimonials from former or current clients for non-advertising purposes in accordance with applicable laws.

5.10 Social Media Channels and Websites
Do not publish info or digital content of clients on your personal social media account and websites.
When publishing info or digital content of clients on your professional social media account and websites, ensure that informed consent was obtained, a disclaimer that it was obtained is included and that the info should not be reused without permission.
Publish in a matter that reduces the potential for sharing, and make efforts to prevent and correct misuse of the shared information.

5.11 Using Digital Content in Public Statement
Before publicly sharing info about clients using digital content ensure informed consent was obtained and include a disclaimer of that.

E-7 Responsibility In Research

6.01 Conforming with Laws and Regulations in Research

Research is any database activity, including analysis of pre-existing data, designed to generate generalizable knowledge for the discipline.

Plan and conduct research following the applicable laws of your state and country.

6.02 Research Review

Conduct research only after approval by a formal research review committee. A committee is a group of professionals that review research proposals to ensure the attic and treatment of human research participants.

6.03 Research in Service Delivery

The client services and welfare are always prioritized and the research activities are arranged the regular service delivery.

Behavior analysts must comply with all ethics requirements for both service delivery and research within the code.

6.04 Informed Consent in Research

Informed consent and assent must be obtained from each individual participating in the research study. Obtain informed consent for the use of data before dissemination, specify that the services will not be impacted by providing or withholding consent, and withdraw consent is possible at any time without penalty.

6.05 Confidentiality in Research

Prioritize the confidentiality of research participants and make appropriate efforts to prevent the accidental sharing of information while conducting research.

6.06 Competence in Conducting Research

Only conduct research independently after you have successfully conducted research under a supervisor in a defined relationship.

Only perform research activities if you are appropriately trained and prepared.

If not competent, seek the appropriate training or collaborate with other professionals.

Behavior analysts are responsible for the ethical conduct of all personnel assigned to the research project.

6.07 Conflict of Interest in Research and Publication

When conducting research identify, disclose, and address conflict of interest.

6.08 Appropriate Credit

Give appropriate credit to all research contributors in all dissemination activities.

6.09 Plagiarism

Do not present another's work or data as your own. Only republish previously published data or text if accompanied by proper disclosure.

6.10 Documentation and Data Retention in Research

Store, transport, retain, and destroy physical and electronic documentation related to research complying with state and country rules.

6.11 Accuracy and Use of Data

Do not fabricate data or falsify results in research.

Data are presented to the public and scientific community in their entirety, whenever possible.

Do not present results that could be misleading or misinterpreted. If you discover errors in published data take steps to correct them.

Coffee and Notes:

F.   **Behavior Assessment**

F-1:   Review records and available data (e.g., educational, medical, historical) at the outset of the case.

F-2:   Determine the need for behavior-analytic services.

F-3:   Identify and prioritize socially significant behavior-change goals.

F-4:   Conduct assessments of relevant skill strengths and deficits.

F-5:   Conduct preference assessments.

F-6:   Describe the common functions of problem behavior.

F-7:   Conduct a descriptive assessment of problem behavior.

F-8:   Conduct a functional analysis of problem behavior.

F-9:   Interpret functional assessment data.

PRONE TO ATTENTION SEEKING BEHAVIOR

F-1 Review Records And Available Data (E.g., Educational, Medical, Historical) At The Outset Of The Case

A behavioral assessment is the first step to identifying the problems/needs of the client before making a plan to change them. It gathers information to make data-based decisions regarding behavior and the environment. It includes indirect and direct procedures such as interviews, checklists, observations, systematic manipulations, and tests to identify the specific target behavior.

4 phases of intervention:
1. Assessment (AKA: Functional Behavior Assessment FBA)
2. Planning
3. Implementing
4. Evaluation

Preliminary Assessment

Informed consent is the first step to complete before implementing a preliminary assessment. It is unethical to review records, complete intake paperwork, or take the case without receiving informed consent for the assessment to be conducted.

Before starting a case, gather information on relevant factors such as medical history, biological history, and education. Review all existing written records and other stored data.

Medical

All medical reasons for suspected unusual behavior should be ruled out before implementing any behavioral intervention that won't work in this case.

E.g., treating "hitting head" as a SIB where the practitioner needs to block every instance and implement an extinction procedure will not work if the child has an ear infection.

Education

Examine past school reports, graphs, treatment plans, IEP, and grades.

E.g., your client has an IEP and receives an hour of speech and OT per week in school.

Historical

We consult prior behavior plans, treatment plans, and skill acquisition plans. We should review what worked and didn't work in the past and understand the client's history.

E.g., what type of reinforcer worked in the past?

F-2 Determine The Need For Behavior-Analytic Services

A preliminary assessment is necessary to gather basic information about a case and determine if behavioral services are desired, needed, and appropriate. Make sure always to have the client and stakeholder consent first! For the BACB, the assessment is an ethical requirement.

To evaluate each case, we can answer the following questions:

- Is the behavior really a problem? Are the behaviors socially significant?
- Is the problem with the client or someone else?
- Are services desired?
- Are the issues enough to require interventions? Does it impact the daily-daily life of the client?
- Is the behavior dangerous to self or others?
- Is the behavior different compared to same-aged, typically developing peers?
- Is ABA the best option? Have medical options been exhausted? It is also necessary to determine if other services are needed or appropriate: medical services, social services, OT, SLP, etc.

Some tools used to determine a need for services include:

- Functional Behavior Assessment
- Observations of the individual
- Review of existing data
- Interview with key supports
- Review of records

Ethically behavior analysts also need to consider the following:

- Does the analyst have time to take on the client?
- Does it have competency? Does the need fall within the scope of the behavior analyst?
- Does the analyst have the resources to take on the case?

Before starting the assessment, consider that the assessment process itself can impact behavior due to reactivity (the presence of the assessor). Reactive effects are usually temporary, so keep assessing.

F-3 Identify And Prioritize Socially Significant Behavior-Change Goals

There is no set method of prioritizing goals for all clients as every client will have their own unique and individual needs. There are, however, some areas of focus that will help guide the decision-making process:

Socially Significant

Skills and behaviors should be socially significant (Applied dimension of ABA).

We consider behaviors that have immediate and long-term benefits, enable the client to contact reinforcement in the natural environment, and are important to the client, the family, and society. Be careful; the changes in behavior must always benefit the individual whose behavior is being targeted first. E.g., the teacher wants the kid to stay still in his chair. This is more important for the teacher than the kid, so it is not socially significant.

When selecting socially significant behavior goals, ask yourself the following questions:

•   After treatment ends, will the behavior produce reinforcement in the client's natural environment (AKA: Relevance of behavior rule)? If yes, the behavior will likely be maintained over time, and the individual will benefit from it.

•   Is this behavior a necessary prerequisite for a useful skill? E.g., teach phonemes as a prerequisite to reading.

•   Will this behavior increase the client's access to environments where other important behaviors can be learned and used?

•   Is this an age-appropriate behavior?

•   Will this behavior lead others to behave more positively toward the client? E.g., taking turns during games will result in friends being nicer with the client and including him during playtime more often.

•   If the proposed target behavior is to be reduced or eliminated, what adaptive behavior will replace it? Never plan to reduce or eliminate a behavior from a person's repertoire without determining an adaptive behavior that will take its place (Fair pair-rule) and designing an intervention plan to ensure that the replacement behavior is learned.

•   Does this behavior pose any danger to the client or others? Safety must always be our priority.

•   How many opportunities will the person have to use this new behavior? How often does this problem behavior occur?

•   Does the behavior produce a lot of negative attention from others?

•   How likely is the success in changing this target behavior?

•   Are there enough resources to change the behavior? Consider the cost-benefit ratio.

•   Is this behavior a behavioral cusp or a pivotal behavior?

•   Choose a behavior and not a goal outcome of behaviors. E.g., passing the exam is not a behavior; it's the outcome goal.

Normalization (AKA: Mainstreaming) is the belief that individuals with disabilities should be physically and socially integrated into mainstream society to the maximum extent possible, and we should promote behaviors that are as culturally "normal" as possible.

E.g., Interacting politely with peers and reducing self-talk are likely behaviors that increase acceptance into the general education classroom.

Habilitation (AKA: Adjustment) occurs when an individual's repertoire has been changed such that short and long-term reinforcers are maximized, and short and long-term punishers are minimized.

Pivotal Behavior

A behavior that, when learned, produces corresponding modifications in other untrained behaviors. (think generalization)

E.g., Giving the client the skill of self-management will allow them more independence in other areas of their life (e.g., navigating the community, chores at home, etc.).

E.g., choice-making, self-management, FCT, eye contact, etc.

Behavioral Cusp

A large significant behavior change that has widespread effects and exposes an individual to new contingencies and reinforcers. Those are high-priority targets.

E.g., reading, walking, driving, toilet training, generalized imitation, etc.

Outcomes

The outcome is what a person wants to accomplish in their life. The goal of our service is to help our clients to reach their outcomes. It doesn't specify any behavior change but only the final goal.

E.g., Living independently in an apartment.

Behavior Categories

Behavior categories lead the individual to obtain the desired outcome. They need to be:

- Socially significant: useful, meaningful to the individual, and that improves the quality of life
- Contextually appropriate: to social norms, to the culture of the individual
- Reachable
- Measurable

E.g., Hygiene, Meal preparation, time management.

Discrete Responses

Discrete responses are specific target behaviors related to the behavior categories and outcomes.

E.g., showering, preparing a sandwich, setting the alarm clock, etc.

E.g., Improve health (outcome), lose 20kg (behavior goal), go to the gym 4 times/week for 1h (target behavior).

F-4 Conduct Assessments Of Relevant Skill Strengths And Deficits

Functional behavior assessment (FBA) is composed by:

- ## Indirect Assessment:
  - Interviews
  - Rating scales (AKA Likert Scales): rate from 1-10, agree/disagree
  - Questionnaires
  - Surveys
  - Checklists

No direct observation. Not reliable because subjective. Use it to identify the client's primary concerns, obtain information from people familiar with the learner, and hypothesize on the maintaining function of behavior.

- ## Direct Assessment:
  - Standardized tests: have scoring tables and charts for plotting results. A Skill Assessment is an evaluation tool used to measure an existing skill set and to provide guidance in determining and planning which skills to target for strengthening or acquisition. We want to assess and measure behavior that the client can already do. It is not a teaching opportunity because we are only observing. Some examples are:
    - o VB-MAPP (Verbal Behavior Milestones Assessment and Placement Program): based on Skinner's analysis of verbal behavior. It contains milestones up to age 4. It helps identify barriers, milestones, placement, IEP goals, teaching format, and educational priorities.
    - o PEAK (Promoting the Emergence of Advanced Knowledge): It assesses the basic and advanced language and cognition skills of children and adults with ASD.
    - o EFL (Essential for Living): assesses communication, problem behavior, and functional skills for individuals with ASD and developmental delays with severe to moderate disabilities and deficits.
    - o AFLS (Assessment of Functional Living Skills): skills are broken down into areas such as home skills, school skills, community participation skills, etc. It focuses on skills people require to function across all environments. It includes skills such as cooking, getting a job, grocery shopping, personal hygiene, bathing, toileting, transportation, community safety skills, etc. Typically this assessment is used with older clients, however, some components of these assessments may be relevant to younger clients as well.
    - o Vineland Adaptive Behavior Scales 3rd edition (Vineland-3)
  - Criterion-referenced assessment: measuring performance based on commonly accepted criteria.
  - Curriculum-based assessment: often used by teachers. It looks at the performance level on specific tasks or lessons. Skill is occurring independently, with help, or not at all.
  - Ecological assessment: looks at the complex environmental relationships of every element of an individual's life. It accesses all settings or times your client engages in challenging behavior. (Not so popular)
  - Descriptive assessment: Observation in the natural environment but no manipulation. They are used to identify events that may be correlated with the behavior, and hypothesis of function. It includes:
    - o Direct observation
    - o ABC Narrative recording
    - o ABC Continuous recording
    - o Scatterplots

- ## Functional Analysis (FA):

Manipulation and environmental arrangements. Empirical demonstration of control. Sometimes not practical or not ethical because it reinforces problem behavior for a period of time. Brief FA could be a solution.

Functional assessment can be viewed as a 4 step process:
1) Gather information with indirect and descriptive assessment
2) Interpret info from step 1) and formulate hypothesis about the function of the problem behavior
3) Test hypothesis using functional analysis (FA)
4) Develop intervention options based on the function of problem behavior

Repertoire - Baseline

Everything that the client already does. Skills strengths are the foundation for other related skills to teach. When conducting a baseline trial, only an SD (e.g., instruction/cue for behavior to occur) should be given unless otherwise stated by your supervisor. If the client is unable to produce the target behavior, the target behavior should not be error corrected unless stated by your supervisor. Additionally, no prompts should be given during a baseline trial unless stated by your supervisor.

When creating individualized programs, it is critical to identify the areas the client is not performing well. Deficits give us critical targets that often include prerequisite behaviors that individual needs to learn to achieve desired goals and outcomes. Why is the skill not happening?

Skill Deficit
- The client doesn't do the skill at all.
- The client doesn't do it independently and needs assistance.
- The client doesn't initiate and needs prompting.

Problem With The Strength Of The Skill
- Lack of mastery, the client doesn't do the skill well.
- Lack of fluency, the client doesn't do the skill fast.
- Lack of frequency, the client doesn't do the skill often enough.

Problem With Occurrence
- Lack of generality, the client does the skill only in limited circumstances.
- Lack of stimulus control, the client does the skill in the wrong place or at the wrong time.
- Lack of compliance/performance problem, the client won't do the skill, but he can do it.

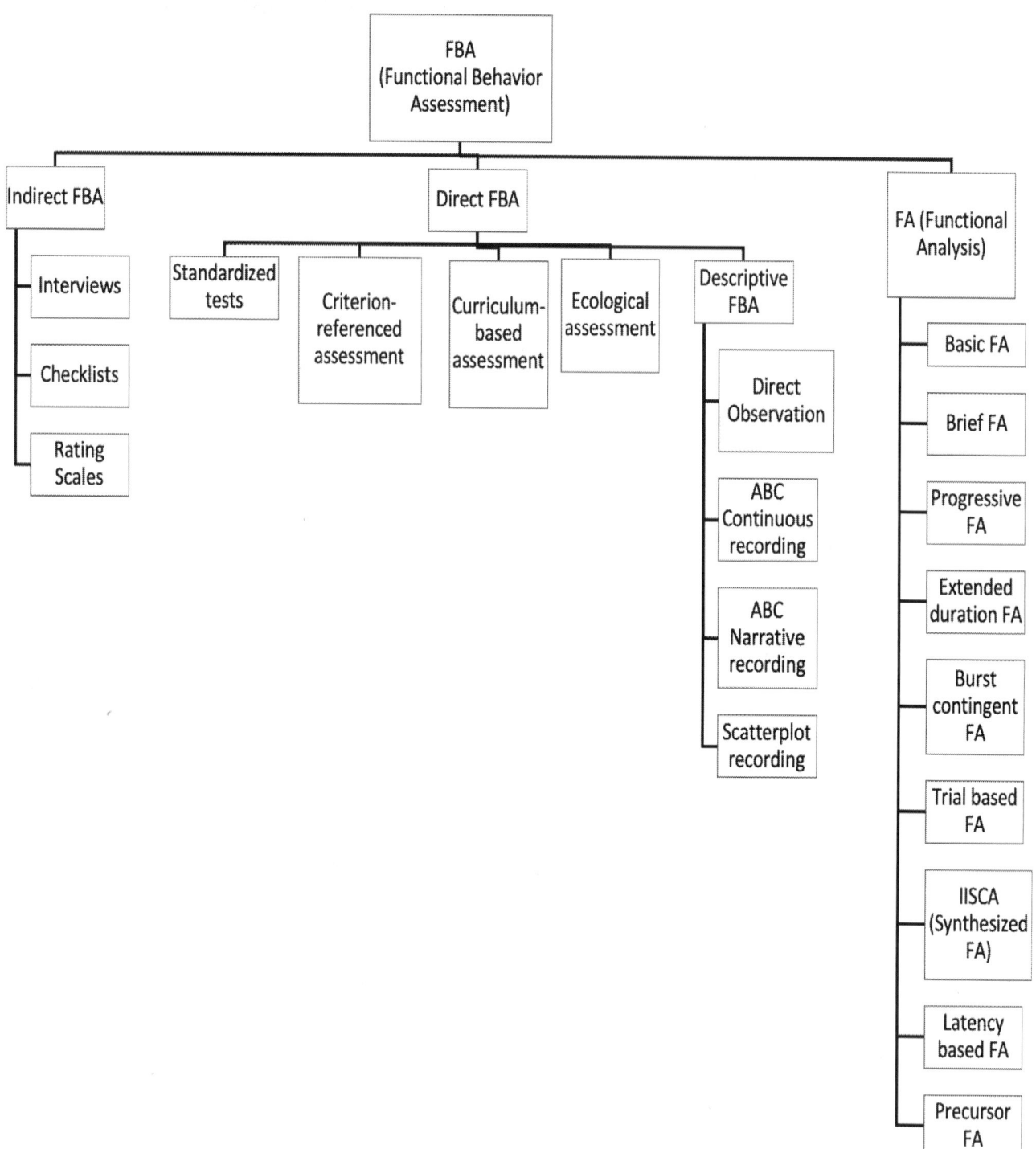

F-5 Conduct Stimulus Preference Assessments (SPA)

A preference assessment is a set of procedures that, depending on the methods, involves some combination of presenting an individual with preferred/potentially preferred stimuli to determine the most-to-least preferred stimuli. The purpose of a preference assessment is to identify potential reinforcers.

Careful: it is NOT a reinforcer assessment! We don't know if these activities/items are reinforcing until we see an increase in behavior over time. Just because something is preferred does not make it a reinforcer.

SPA are generally simple to conduct and do not require a high response effort for the participant; for example, the individual only has to reach for the item to access it.

Here are some ways to identify a potential reinforcer:

Indirect Preference Assessments

It's an informant-based assessment that provides information about preferences using interviews, open-ended questions, checklists, and rating scales. They can be completed by the client, caregivers, or significant others. It should always be used as a first step to start.

Free Operant (Naturalistic Or Contrived Observation)

This assessment involves a variety of preferred and potentially preferred stimuli set out and available for the client in their natural environment.

The clinician would record which item(s) the client interacts with and the total duration of the interaction. The client can freely choose which stimuli to engage with, and the clinician is asked not to engage with the client at this time. The stimuli are ranked by the frequency of selections and the time the client spent with them. The longer they engage with the stimulus, the stronger the item is preferred.

Trial Based SPA

Stimuli are presented in a series of trials. Responses to the stimuli are measured by looking at the client's behavior. These includes:

- Single stimulus
- Paired stimuli
- Multiple stimuli

Single Stimulus

One single stimulus is presented for a period of time, and the person's reaction, approach, and engagement with it are noted. Engagement behaviors include touching, playing with, looking at, and holding the item. After a set time, the item is removed, and a new stimulus is presented. This is helpful for individuals who may have trouble choosing between two or more items.

Paired Stimuli (AKA: Forced Choice)

Simultaneous presentation of 2 items (presentation in pairs). Each stimulus is matched randomly with all other stimuli. The learner's choice of the two is recorded. We can rank order all the items and the item chosen the most times is the highest in the preference assessment.

This method takes a lot of time to implement but is the most accurate because it creates a hierarchy.

E.g., Present an iPad and a toy car to your client and have him choose one item. Once the client makes a selection, allow them to engage with the item for about 30-60 seconds.

Multiple Stimuli

Many items (3 or more) are presented in an array simultaneously.

• **Multiple Stimuli with Replacement (MSWR):** a variety of potentially preferred stimuli are set out and available for the client. The clinician would record which item the client interacts with. The client can engage with the stimulus for about 30-60 seconds. Selected items are put back into the array, and the array can be interspersed (i.e., moved around) to avoid any positional/selection biases. The client can choose which stimuli to engage with freely and continue to select the exact same stimulus if they decide to do so. The stimuli with a high frequency of selection would be considered most preferred.

• **Multiple Stimuli without Replacement (MSWO):** a variety of potentially preferred stimuli are available for the client. The clinician would record which item the client interacts with. The client can engage with the stimuli for about 30-60 seconds. Selected items are not put back into the array, and the array can be interspersed (i.e., moved around) to avoid any positional/selection biases. The client can choose which stimuli to engage with freely and cannot choose an already selected stimulus as it is no longer present. The stimuli selected first in order are considered to be most preferred.

Note: the item chosen first is taken out of the array and the array diminishes in size on each selection. You will always be left with 1 item. The same item can't be chosen more than one time.

Type of PA	# of items presented	Advantages	Limitations
Indirect assessment	Tools: Interview, checklists, rating scales, survey	Simple Efficient Narrows the field	Subjective Unreliable Self-report require verbal skills
Free operant	All the ones available in the environment	No demand No verbal repertoire required No problem behavior	False-negative (only one item used but others are possible reinforcers) Possible limited access to stimuli in the environment No hierarchy
Single stimulus	1	Simple No scan required	Undifferentiated approach (false positive) Removal of the item

Type of PA	# of items presented	Advantages	Limitations
Paired stimulus	2	More sensitive that SS Establish hierarchy	Time consuming Position bias (selection based on the position of the item, not his preference) False negative (not selecting items that are reinforcers)
MSWR	More than 3 Item return to the array after being selected. Intersperse items.	Efficient Provide info about most preferred	No info about the items not being selected Scan skill required
MSWO	More than 3 The item selected is removed from the array. Array diminishes.	Provide info about all items	Removal of the item could cause problem behavior. The first choice could not be the most preferred, sometimes we leave the best at the end.

Note for selecting items:
- Assess food and leisure items separately
- Select stimuli that are a good ecological fit

Considerations:
- Preferences change
- Methods can be combined
- Verify if stimulus preferences are actually reinforcers (see below)

Reinforcer Assessment (AKA Reinforcer Analysis)

The technique is used to evaluate the effectiveness of a stimulus as a reinforcer and follows the preference assessment.

Behavior is measured when the stimulus is provided contingent on behavior and when it's not provided. If the stimulus is, in fact, a reinforcer, we expect an increase in the future occurrence of the behavior. There are different types of reinforcement assessment:

- **Concurrent Schedule**: identifies what contingency is most effective as a reinforcer when 2 responses are available at the same time, and a different consequence is available for the completion of each response. Responses are similar and are available simultaneously to provide a choice. Think about the Matching Law. E.g., put the block in the box on the left to get a candy, or put the block in the box on the right to get chips.

E.g., read 10 pages of a book to get 10 min TV time, or read 20 pages to get 20 min TV time.

• **In-the-Moment Reinf. Analysis**: make an in-the-moment decision about what stimulus/potential reinforcer to deliver contingent on desired target behavior, considering the client's facial expression and affect. E.g., the client is looking at the Pokemon cards I have on my desk and he's smiling. So when he completes his math exercise, I give him the cards. I then observe and record if his math exercise completion increases over time.

• **Multiple Schedule**: identifies what contingency is most effective as a reinforcer when 2 or more components schedules are available on 1 behavior, with only 1 schedule in effect at a time. An SD signals which schedule is in effect.

• **Progressive Ratio Schedule**: reinforcer effectiveness is assessed as the response requirement increases up to a breakpoint. It gives us info about the strength of the reinforcer. The more effort it sustains, the more powerful the reinforcer is.
E.g., For 1 math question completed, I give 1 candy to the client. I then progressively increase the amount of work to meet (2 math questions, 3, 4, and so on) to receive the same candy, only 1. The client stopped completing the math questions when 3 were required. (Breaking point)

F-6 Describe The Common Functions Of Problem Behavior

All behavior happens for a reason; the function is why it occurs and maintains over time. The practitioner develops individualized treatments based on the function of the behavior.
The four functions of behavior are:

- **Access to Attention**: Attention-maintained behaviors have a social mediation component (i.e., to get another person's attention). A critical note about attention-maintained behaviors is that the individual engaging in the behavior may look for positive and/or negative attention. For example, they may rip up their worksheet to receive a verbal reprimand or throw an item across a classroom to get other students to laugh. In general, most interventions would focus on teaching the client a replacement skill to access attention in more appropriate ways (i.e., functional communication training FCT).
E.g., A child whines when his mom is talking to her friend. Teach him to say, "Mom, look!" or to tap her shoulder.

- **Escape-Maintained Behavior**: Escape-maintained behaviors typically look like an individual trying to get out of an expectation, task, situation, people, aversive sensory stimulation, or environment. This may appear as physically leaving an environment (e.g., leaving their work area), destroying property (e.g., ripping their worksheet), refusing to participate (e.g., not responding to a question), etc. In most scenarios, some form of follow-through is typically recommended to help reduce escape-maintained behaviors and provide a functional replacement skill (e.g., asking for a break, asking to come back to it later, etc.). Individuals typically engage in escape to access something (e.g., another activity, free time, an item, etc.); however, escape-maintained behaviors can also be used to remove an aversive.
E.g., A child tears up a math worksheet, and the teacher puts him in time out.

- **Access to Tangibles or Activities**: Access to tangible maintained behaviors includes behaviors that allow access to a preferred item/activity or attempt to access these items/activities. This definition does encompass a large variety of items/activities such as food items, toys, games, technology, environments, equipment, etc. In general, most interventions will focus on teaching the client a replacement skill to gain access to these items/activities (e.g., functional communication training) and to teach a combination of tolerating denial, delayed, and denied access to these items/activities.
E.g., A child cries at the grocery store, and his mom buys him candies.

- **Automatic/Sensory Maintained Behaviors**: Automatic maintained behaviors tend to occur across all situations and environments. These are also perhaps one of the more complex functions to determine as these behaviors may serve a purpose that is not observable or measurable (e.g., a client feeling itchy due to specific material). In general, interventions typically focus on providing the client with an appropriate way to access their sensory needs (e.g., providing a client with a stress ball seeking deep pressure with their hands). Another alternative may be providing functional communication or a more appropriate replacement skill.
E.g., the child flaps his hands. We give him a slime to play with instead.

All behaviors are maintained by one or more of the four functions of behavior.
Attention, escape, and access to tangible are socially mediated, meaning that other people are required to provide the reinforcers.
Sensory stimulation is automatic, meaning that it occurs without the presentation of consequences by other people.

Behavior is maintained by:

•   Positive reinforcement (Social attention, access to tangible and sensory/automatic): behavior evoked by the absence of an appetitive condition.

•   Negative reinforcement (Escape and sensory/automatic): behavior evoked by the presence of an aversive condition.

F-7 Conduct A Descriptive Assessment Of Problem Behavior

Descriptive assessment is a method in which behavior is directly observed and measured in a real-life context without manipulating environmental variables. We observe a variety of situations and then record events that proceed and follow problem behavior to identify patterns and the possible function of a target behavior. There are different types:

ABC Narrative Recording (Aka: Sequence Analysis, Abc Descriptive Data)
It's a written description of the individual's behaviors and the environmental conditions under which those behaviors occur over a period of time. Open-ended blank ABC data sheet.

ABC Continuous Recording
It is one of the most common data collection methods used to determine the behavior's function. An observer records all occurrences of the specific target behavior, antecedents and consequences on checklists during a specific period of time (20/30 min).

Scatterplot (AKA: Pattern Analysis)
It's a data collection form for recording the times of day during which a target behavior has occurred, typically involving dividing the days into blocks of time. It helps to compare contexts in which behavior does and does not occur. It analyzes patterns of behavior.

These assessment methods allow you to develop hypotheses about the antecedent and consequence variables controlling the problem behavior. Still, they do not prove that the variables are functionally related to the behavior.

F-8 Conduct a Functional Analysis Of Problem Behavior

Functional analysis FA (AKA: Experimental Analysis, Analog Assessment)

It is the process of identifying environmental events that are functionally related to behavior by systematically manipulating antecedents and consequences and measuring behavior under different conditions.

The functional analysis provides information on why problem behavior occurs and helps you determine appropriate treatments.

Ethical concerns: during functional analysis, we want the problem behavior to occur and deliver reinforcement contingent on that target behavior.

Collect data on behavior during the different conditions and use a multielement design to graph them. We are comparing the control (free-play) condition with the test conditions and looking for a separation in the data path. A function is determined when the target behavior increases under certain environmental conditions. Repeat the test and control conditions to demonstrate experimental control using a random sequence or the alone-attention-play-demand sequence.

E.g., elevated problem behavior in the contingent attention condition suggests that problem behavior is maintained by social positive reinforcement.

E.g., during the demand condition, the client would be given an escape from the demand if they engaged in the target behavior (e.g., throwing a worksheet). If this behavior increases during this condition, the data may support escape as the function of the target behavior.

Condition	Antecedent	Behavior	Consequence
Free Play: Control condition	- Enriched environment - Preferred items/activities available for free access - No demands - Lots of attention from the clinician	Problem behavior should not happen or be very low	Problem behavior is ignored
Attention or Social disapproval: testing for social SR+	- Therapist present - Attention is removed or placed on something else	Challenging behavior occurs	- When problem behavior occurs, provide attention for a brief time (reprimands, soothing statement, eye contact, touch, expression). - Ignore all other behaviors, including appropriate ones.
Tangible: testing for social SR+ (Only test if needed)	- Therapist present - Withhold of the preferred item/food/activity	Challenging behavior occurs	- When problem behavior occurs, deliver the preferred item/food/activity for a brief time.

Condition	Antecedent	Behavior	Consequence
Escape or Academic demand: testing for social SR-	- Therapist present - Lots of demands are placed	Challenging behavior occurs	- When problem behavior occurs, the demands are removed - Ignore all other behaviors
Alone: test for sensory, automatic reinforcer	- Austere environment, no toys, no food - No therapist present - Client is alone	Challenging behavior occurs	Problem behavior is ignored, no social contingency arranged.

E.g., FA determined that the function of the behavior is attention as shown in the graph below.

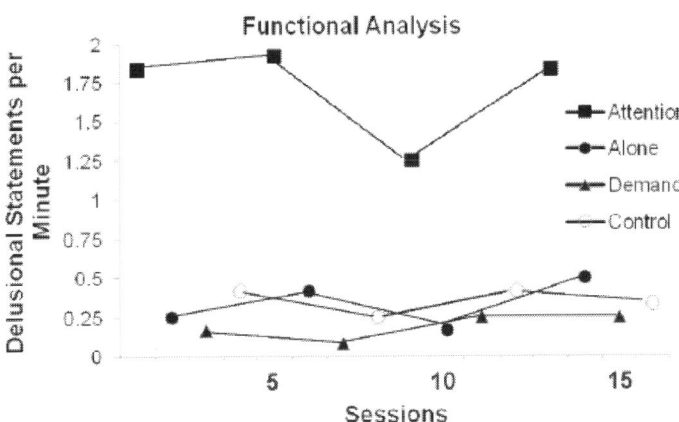

FA Modification For High-Risk Behavior

One of the most common barriers to an FA is that people don't think it is safe or ethically appropriate to conduct it with high-risk behaviors. FA may temporarily increase the behavior and reinforce it during the treatment, but if not done, the client could be exposed to prolonged ineffective treatments.

Some of the following modifications can be made:

• Protective equipment. E.g., helmet

• Blocking: physically preventing the completion of the response

• Precursor FA: provide the reinforcer for the precursor behavior. Target behavior should decrease since it already has received the reinforcer.

E.g., yelling always occurs before hitting behavior. Provide reinforcers for yelling; the hitting should decrease if they have the same function.

• Latency FA: allow target behavior to occur only once and measure the time between the start of the trial when the EO is in place and the first occurrence of the behavior. The condition with the shorter time indicates the likely function of the behavior.

FA Modification For Lack Of Space

Trial-based FA: In the natural environment, intersperse short trials of different conditions, allowing the target behavior to occur only once per condition. Compare the % of trials where the behavior occurred and not occurred.

FA Modification For Lack Of Time

•   Brief FA: few short sessions are conducted, so we have an abbreviated form of the standard functional analysis. 1 or 2 sessions of 5-10 min for each FA condition. It can also be used if the behavior is very severe.

•   Progressive FA: prior to conducting the FA, we eliminate some conditions to shorten the assessment.

FA Modification For Low Rates Behavior

•   Extended duration FA: conduct long sessions for each condition, up to 7h long.

•   Burst contingent: FA starts contingent on the target behavior. The observation is not continuous but only begins when the problem behavior occurs.

IISCA (AKA Synthesized FA)

Interview-informed synthesized contingent analysis is a variation of the FA.

This method can be used when we suspect the behavior has multiple control, several contingencies are affecting the behavior. We only test the contingencies that, from the interview, resulted in possible functions of the behavior.

In the test condition, multiple contingencies are implemented simultaneously (E.g., attention, and escape) when the problem behavior occurs. In the control condition, the same contingencies are presented non-contingently and continuously.

Look for clear different patterns between test and control conditions.

F-9 Interpret Functional Assessment Data

Collecting Data
Depending on the method used to conduct your functional assessment, it is important to have data representative of what you require to determine the function of the target behavior. Data is what allows us to analyze and determine patterns.

Visual Analysis
This is perhaps the most common way of analyzing data. Once data is collected, it can be graphed and visually inspected to determine patterns which leads to determining a function.
You have an obligation to collect and graphically display data in a manner that allows for decisions and recommendations for behavior change program development.

Determining The Function
- If problem behavior occurred during the control condition this may indicate undifferentiated results, inconclusive results, or an issue with the implementation of the functional analysis.
- If problem behavior occurred in the alone condition, the function may be sensory/automatic reinforcement.
- If problem behavior occurred in the tangible condition, the function may be access to tangible.
- If problem behavior occurred in the demand condition, the function may be escape.
- If problem behavior occurred in the attention condition, the function may be access to attention.
- Undifferentiated response patterns between conditions could mean:
    - Multiple control (more than one variable is maintaining the behavior)
    - Automatic is the function of behavior
    - Relevant variables were not tested
    - Discrimination difficulties
    - Behavior has different topographies that have different functions.

E.g., tantrum behavior is defined as kicking (function is escape) and screaming (function is attention).

It is important to note that behavior can have more than one function.

Conditional Probability
Conditional Probability is a score from 0 to 1 that calculates the possibility that a target behavior will occur under specific circumstances. It is calculated from any ABC data and is used to hypothesize the function of behavior. Be careful; it can be misleading. The formula is:
# of behaviors proceeded by a specific antecedent and or followed by a specific consequence divided by the Tot # of observed behaviors.
It is always reported in decimals; it cannot exceed 1.0, and the closer it is to 1.0, the stronger the probability.
E.g., 0.8 is stronger than 0.2 probability.
E.g., After analyzing the ABC data, we noticed that 3 out of 4 instances of challenging behavior occurred after a demand was placed. 1 out of 4 instances of challenging behavior occurred after a tangible was removed. ¾= 0.75 and ¼=0.25, so there is a stronger probability that the client will engage in challenging behavior after placing a demand.

Coffee and Notes:

Shhh...

G. Behavior-Change Procedures

G-1:   Use positive and negative reinforcement procedures to strengthen behavior.

G-2:   Use interventions based on motivating operations and discriminative stimuli.

G-3:   Establish and use conditioned reinforcers

G-4:   Use stimulus and response prompts and fading (e.g., errorless, most-to-least, least-to-most, prompt delay, stimulus fading).

G-5:   Use modeling and imitation training.

G-6:   Use instructions and rules.

G-7:   Use shaping.

G-8:   Use chaining.

G-9:   Use discrete-trial, free-operant, and naturalistic teaching arrangements.

G-10:   Teach simple and conditional discriminations.

G-11:   Use Skinner's analysis to teach verbal behavior.

G-12:   Use equivalence-based instruction.

G-13:   Use the high-probability instructional sequence.

G-14:   Use reinforcement procedures to weaken behavior (e.g., DRA, FCT, DRO, DRL, NCR).

G-15:   Use extinction.

G-16:   Use positive and negative punishment (e.g., time-out, response cost, overcorrection).

G-17:   Use token economies.

G-18:   Use group contingencies.

G-19:   Use contingency contracting.

G-20:   Use self-management strategies.

G-21: Use procedures to promote stimulus and response generalization.

G-22: Use procedures to promote maintenance.

It's all
fun and games
until someone figures
out the function
of your
BEHAVIOR

G-1 Use Positive And Negative Reinforcement Procedures To Strengthen Behavior

View Task List B-4

Positive Reinforcement

An operant (learned) behavior contingency in which a behavior is emitted, a stimulus is added to the environment, and as a result, the behavior is more likely to happen in the future. Positive is used to mean adding" something when the behavior occurs (such as giving a child a sticker when they clean their room) and reinforcement refers to the increased probability of that behavior happening again in the future (the kid cleans their room more often as a result of the added sticker).

Negative Reinforcement

Negative reinforcement is a consequence following a behavior that involves removing someone or one's self from an aversive situation. By removing an aversive, it increases the future frequency of behavior. The two types of negative reinforcement are escape and avoidance. An example of negative reinforcement is taking a tylenol to remove your headache. The relief experienced here results in you taking tylenol the next time you have a headache or an ache.

Premack Principle (AKA: Grandma's Law)

It is usually stated as "First...then..."; this strategy uses behavior as a reinforcer. Your client will complete a low-rate behavior (something less likely to do) before doing a high-rate behavior. It is used to complete nonpreferred tasks.

E.g., First, brush your teeth, then you can watch TV.

E.g., First, complete the math worksheet, then you can go to play outside.

G-2 Use Interventions Based On Motivating Operations And Discriminative Stimuli

Motivating operations (MO) and Discriminative Stimuli (SD) are both antecedent variables that alter the current frequency of a behavior.

Discriminative Stimuli (view Task List B-10)
An SD influences behavior because it has been correlated with a history of reinforcer in its presence and not in its absence. Interventions based on discriminative stimuli will alter the rate, latency, duration, or magnitude of behavior based on the presence or absence of the discriminative stimulus.
E.g., the rat receives food for lever presses when the light is on and never when the light is off. The light functions as SD; it signals the availability of food as a reinforcer.

Motivating Operation (view Task List B-12)
MO-->SD-->R-->C (4 terms contingency)
This is an environmental variable that momentarily alters the effectiveness of a stimulus as a reinforcer or punisher.
E.g., a child sees a box of pizza sitting on the counter and requests a slice of pizza.
An MO can establish or abolish the value of a reinforcer and so evoke or abate behavior.
An MO controls behavior because the relevant consequence has been more effective in its presence than in its absence.
E.g., the rat would press the lever only when the light is on (SD) and when he is hungry (MO for food deprivation). If the rat is food satiated, the reinforcer is less effective but still available (it's not extinction).

In non-technical terms, the SD tells you that something you want is available, and the MO makes you want something.

Antecedent Interventions
Antecedent interventions are implemented prior to and independent of the occurrence of the target behavior (Not contingent on behavior). Some are used to manipulate the MO to make the behavior more or less effortful.
3 types of antecedent interventions are:

NCR
Noncontingent reinforcement is an antecedent intervention in which stimuli with known reinforcing properties are delivered independently of the behavior at a time interval (FT or VT).
The reinforcer that maintains behavior is provided frequently and freely, so there is no need to engage in the behavior. It's an abolishing operation (AO) that reduces the motivation to engage in the behavior.
NCR requires the identification of the function in order to choose NCR with positive, negative, or automatic SR. We need to conduct an FBA to establish the maintaining consequence of the challenging behavior, then collect a baseline to establish the NCR schedule. Make sure the NCR schedule is thicker than what typically maintains the behavior.
E.g., Luca cries every 5 min to get attention from his mom. Mom will deliver attention every 4 min. This decreased Luca's behavior.
NCR is easy to implement and is often used in treatment packages. A downside is that it doesn't teach appropriate or new behaviors to the client.

High Probability Instructional Sequence/High-P (view Task List G-13)

It's an antecedent intervention where 2/5 easy tasks, called high-p, are presented in quick succession before requesting the target task, the low-p.

FCT

Functional communication training establishes an appropriate communicative behavior to replace problem behaviors evoked by an MO. It develops communicative behaviors using the DRA procedure to teach an adaptive response that produces the same reinforcer. Note that the new response needs to have the same function as the challenging behavior.

It can be vocal, signs, picture cards, gestures, etc.

Initially, use the FR1 schedule of reinforcement for the new communicative response. Consider using it in a treatment package.

G-3 Establish and Use Conditioned Reinforcers (AKA: Secondary Reinforcers)

View task list B-8

Conditioned reinforcers are stimuli with no innate properties that serve as reinforcement after being paired with another unconditioned reinforcer or conditioned reinforcer.

Conditioned reinforcers enable us to use a variety of stimuli as reinforcers (like praise, activities, people, toys, candies, etc.). Remember to do a reinforcer assessment for every individual.

G-4 Use Stimulus And Response Prompts And Fading (E.G., Errorless, Most-To-Least, Least-To-Most, Prompt Delay, Stimulus Fading)

Prompt

A prompt is a temporary supplemental stimulus that increases the likelihood of the target response and reduces the chances of errors.

Prompts are individualized for each client and every program. We should always implement the least intrusive prompt and plan for fading it over time. It should be used prior to or during the desired response. They should always be temporary: be careful of prompt dependency!

Response Prompts

Response prompts operate directly on the behavior to cue a correct response. They do not change the task or the stimuli. There are different types of response prompt:

• Verbal instructions: additional instruction that we want eventually to remove. It's different from the SD, which always controls the response. It can be vocal, or written, with pictures or sounds. E.g., an alarm that rings as a reminder, the written instructions for completing a task, vocally reminding the client to go to the bathroom. This can be used as a full verbal prompt (i.e., giving the client the verbal response) or as a partial verbal prompt (i.e., giving the client the beginning sound of the verbal response). For example, a full verbal prompt would be holding up a picture of a lion and saying "lion." An example of a partial verbal prompt would be holding up the image of the lion and saying "li...".

• Modeling: demonstration of the correct response by the practitioner, effective for clients that can imitate. This prompt requires attending skills to copy the instructor demonstrating the target behavior.
E.g., if you are teaching a child how to kick a soccer ball, the instructor would give the instruction "kick" and then model kicking the ball. The child will then imitate.

• Physical guidance: The trainer physically guides the client through the motions to complete the response. It can be full physical (hand over hand) or partial (tap shoulder/touch elbow/touch the wrist). Physical prompts are perhaps one of the most intrusive prompts and are typically faded as quickly as possible. It also doesn't offer many opportunities for independence.

Stimulus Prompts

Stimulus prompts operate directly on the antecedent to cue a correct response in conjunction with the critical SD. You want to call the client's attention to the stimulus and direct his behavior. There are 2 types:

• Position prompt: the item taught is placed closer to the client. For example, if you have an array of three pictures in front of the client, you would place the target response closest to them (e.g., if you ask them to "find bike", you would put the picture of the bike closest to them).

• Movement of the stimulus: cueing the client toward the correct response (pointing to the correct card, touching, looking at, tapping the object)

• Redundancy prompt: highlights some characteristics of the controlling stimulus (color, size, amount, transparency, emphasis of the voice)

Errorless Learning

A technique designed to prevent or minimize errors that occur during teaching. It uses prompts to ensure the client meets the target response, so the prompt becomes the SD. We must plan for a prompt fading procedure and promote independence.

It is mainly used when introducing new skills or when errors increase problem behavior and frustration.

E.g., if you say "touch car," you would block and redirect any attempts at touching the ball and prompt touching the car.

E.g., teaching a child to clap their hands, the clinician would deliver the instruction "clap hands" and then fully prompt the child to do so and reinforce. As the clinician continues to deliver trials, the amount of prompting would eventually be faded out.

Most-To-Least Prompting (AKA Maximum to Minimum)
A procedure in which the learner is physically guided to complete the response requirement, and the amount of physical guidance is reduced across trials as teaching progresses.

It is used when teaching new skills and when errors evoke problem behavior.

We start at the least intrusive and most effective prompt, then fade it over time.

The hierarchy is: full physical- partial physical- model- verbal - natural cue (SD).

E.g., you ask the client to wash their hands and begin teaching it with a hand-over-hand prompt. You then gradually fade it and move to a modeling prompt until the client washes his hands without support.

Least-To-Most Prompting (AKA Minimum to Maximum)
A procedure that allows the learner to perform the response with the least amount of help on each trial and increases until the learner engages in the correct target response. The hierarchy is the opposite of most to least prompting, starting with using the verbal prompt. It is used when the client shows rapid acquisition rates and when there is a performance problem (won't do instead of can't do). The client always has the opportunity to do the skill independently at first, while the prompts are added only based on incorrect responses.

If you are unfamiliar with the client, start with this prompt sequence.

Graduated Guidance
Physical prompting is provided only when necessary, and then faded immediately after. It is a less structured approach that allows for more flexibility. We encourage the learner to perform independently and only intervene when needed. The trainer is in a ready position to prompt immediately if necessary.

Time Delay (AKA: Prompt Delay)
It involves changing when the prompt is presented to allow the client to respond independently. The time between the SD and the prompt increases over time, but the prompt type remains the same. There are two types of prompt delay: constant (delay is the same) and progressive (delay gradually increase).

E.g., you ask the client to wash their hands, wait briefly for them to start the sequence, and if they don't after about 3 seconds, you gesture towards the tap.

Stimulus Fading
It removes the prompt systematically to transfer control to the real SD. It prevents prompt dependency.

E.g., if a child is learning to draw a straight line and when initially teaching the skill, a bold line is used to trace a straight line. Stimulus fading would reduce the boldness of that line until it is completely gone so that the child is able to draw a straight line when instructed to do so.

Stimulus Shaping (AKA: Stimulus Shape Transformation)
Systematically and gradually transform the physical shape of the stimulus prompt to become the natural SD as the client responds correctly. E.g., the prompt is the shape of a heart that gradually changes form into the word "heart" so the client will read it.

G-5 Use Modeling And Imitation Training

Imitation

Imitation is when a learner produces an identical response, or approximately topographically close, to a modeled antecedent stimulus. Imitation is a powerful tool that promotes the quick acquisition of behaviors.

An imitative response must occur without learning history to be defined as an imitation.

There are 3 types of imitation:

1) Motor imitation: movement of body parts. It can be divided in

- Fine motor. It involves movements of the hands and fingers.

- Gross motor. It involves movements of large muscles or the whole body.

- Oral motor. It involves facial movements.

2) Object imitation: movement of an item, how to use it

3) Vocal imitation: sound produced by the mouth, also called echoic

Important features:

- Formal Similarity: model and behavior have the same sense mode, and they physically look alike.

- Model: the stimulus that is being imitated

- Immediacy: an imitative behavior must immediately follow the model

- Controlled Relation: the model must be the controlling variable for imitation

Imitation training steps:
- Assess for prerequisite skills or teach them if necessary
- Select models: range of behaviors to model. Consider developmental sequence and appropriateness of behaviors
- Pretest if the client can imitate some behaviors without training
- Select imitative targets
- Conduct imitation training: provide a model, provide physical assistance as needed, reinforce response, intersperse trials with other mastered skills

Antecedent: "Do this/watch me/your turn" and model
Prompt: physical if necessary, then fade gradually
Consequence: reinforce

Note: True imitation is evoked by a nonverbal SD, not evoked by "copy me" verbal instruction.

Possible problems:
- Slow or no progress: verify if target behavior is appropriate, verify if prerequisite skills are present
- Scrolling (guessing the answer): immediately block errors and increase the amount of guidance
- Faulty stimulus control (emitting a behavior regardless of the model): teach more than one behavior at a time and ensure the client is attending prior to modeling

Generalized Imitation

Imitation of a large range of behaviors without training. The client can imitate novel actions. It's our goal!

Model

A model is an antecedent stimulus that evokes an imitative response, it's what is being imitated. It can be planned or unplanned.

• Unplanned models: not prearranged procedures. Potentially all antecedent stimuli could evoke imitation in everyday social environments. E.g., when in a new city, I follow where people go to take the bus because I don't know.

• Planned models: a prearranged antecedent stimulus that facilitates new skills. E.g. I am taking a class to learn Spanish, I imitate the teacher's words.

The model can be live or symbolic (like a picture, photo, video, or audio).

It is recommended that the model and the client share some similarities. Make sure to present the model in re-al-life scenarios, provide feedback and present many practice opportunities to the client.

G-6 Use Instructions And Rules

Contingency Shaped Behavior (AKA: Contingency Control)

It's a behavior that is shaped through direct contact, and experience with environmental contingencies. You directly experience the consequence of the response and this change your future behavior. Learn from doing. The consequence must occur within 0-30 sec following the response.

E.g., I took out a pan from the oven without gloves. In the future, I'll be more likely to wear gloves when taking out pans from the oven.

E.g., I am bringing a jacket to the office after being cold the last time.

Rule Governed Behavior (AKA: Rules, Rule Control Contingency specifying stimuli-CSS, Rules)

The behavior is primarily controlled by a verbal description (rules, laws, and instructions) of an antecedent-behavior-consequence contingency. There is no obvious consequence for the behavior, or at least we never experience it. Also useful when the consequences are too delayed to influence the behavior directly.

It can be learned faster and may prevent harmful or dangerous consequences.

E.g., Ronnie does not run in the hallway because her teacher taught her that is a school rule.

E.g., My mom told me to use gloves when taking out pans from the oven to not get burned.

E.g., My boss told me to bring a jacket to the office because it's cold. (I didn't experience being cold there, I follow the rule)

E.g., There is a "danger, high voltage" sign on a fence. We do not need to touch the fence to understand that we will get shocked.

E.g., No loitering.

Factors affecting the rules:

1) Specificity: explicit (clear) or implicit rule (unclear)

2) Accuracy: accurate (the consequence follows the rule) or inaccurate (faulty rules. E.g., "Turn left and there is a bar," and when you turn, there isn't a bar)

3) Complexity: the greater the complexity of the rule, the less effective the rule

4) Who provides the rule: self or another person

5) Timing of the rule: immediate or delayed consequence

6) Learner's history: correspondence between the rule and the consequence. E.g., If you study 30min a day, you pass the exam. If you pass the exam, you are more likely to follow this rule in the future.

Rules are most effective when they are explicit, accurate, less complex, self-generated, followed by immediate consequences, and when there is correspondence with contingencies.

Rules should be simple and short, delivered positively (E.g., sit nicely vs. don't move), and must be used in the same way by everyone around the client.

Instructions

Instructions are the steps to learn a skill, complete a task, or reach the desired result. They are response prompts that tell you what to do and reduce the need for instructions in the future.

E.g., instruction in a manual/on a worksheet/ following a recipe.

G-7 Use Shaping

Shaping is a strategy that uses differential reinforcement to gradually change the topography of a response or a response dimension. The process is to reinforce successive approximations to the desired target response and put other behaviors that are less similar to what we want in extinction, until we reach the target behavior.

E.g., to teach to say "Bubble," we may start by teaching to say "B" first and reinforce correct responses, then "Bub," then "Bubbl," and finally "Bubble."

Steps:

•   Operationally defined target behavior and the terminal response mastery criterion (e.g., specific duration, specific magnitude, correct topography, etc.).

•   Determine the baseline level or current level of producing the target behavior.

•   List all of the steps of the target behavior (i.e., task analysis) and determine the success criterion.

•   Teach the skill and differentially reinforce the independence of the current step. Minimize any extraneous stimuli or distractions.

•   When the current step is mastered, put this step on extinction and differentially reinforce the next step.

•   Continue until reaching the terminal response. Plan for generalization and maintenance.

The process is time-consuming, and the practitioner needs to attend closely. Make sure to spend enough time on each step and go back if necessary because progress is not always linear. If the criterion for reinforcing the step is too low, an excessive number of responses will be reinforced; if the criterion is set too high, extinction occurs, and responses do not meet the reinforcer.

Shaping can be:

•   Across response topographies: the topography of behavior changes during shaping. Behaviors are still members of the same response class, but the response form changes and each approximation differs from the others.

E.g., A speech therapist teaches novel vocalization to an individual who does not possess any vocal abilities.

•   Within response topographies: the topography of behavior remains constant, but another measurable dimension of behavior is changed (duration, rate, latency, magnitude, volume).

E.g., the duration of time spent practicing piano increased via shaping.

E.g., The child's voice is too loud, so we are reinforcing gradually lower volumes of voice tone.

Note shaping vs. fading:

Shaping changes the response requirement, while fading changes the antecedent stimulus.

Shhh...

G-8 Use Chaining

Chaining is a procedure that may be used to teach a chain, usually by teaching one step at a time. Each response of the chain is associated with a particular SD, must be performed in order and close in time, and leads to a specific SR.

A behavior chain is created using a task analysis that breaks down a complex behavior into small, teachable steps of the chain. You can perform a task analysis by doing the task yourself or watching someone else competent do the task, but it must be individualized to the client.

Chaining is very important in increasing independent living skills and building more complex and adaptive repertoires.

E.g., When putting toothpaste on a toothbrush, scrubbing your teeth, rinsing your mouth, and putting your toothbrush away are all linked together, they make a behavior chain that represents toothbrushing.

Some examples of behavior chains may include dressing routines, washing hands, shower routine, brushing teeth, etc.

There are 4 different types of chaining procedures:
1. **Backward Chaining**: a procedure in which a response in a chain is taught one at a time, beginning with the last step in the chain, and all the other steps are prompted. The learner contacts the natural reinforcement contingencies during every learning trial at the end of the chain. It is mainly used for self-care skills. E.g., For washing hands: the client is given the opportunity to complete step 7 - turn off the tap. The first 6 steps in the sequence are taught errorlessly. As the client masters the last step, they are then given an independent opportunity to produce the step before that (i.e., step 6). This continues in a backward fashion until the entire chain is taught.

2. **Backward Chaining With Leaps Ahead**: same as Backward chaining, but some steps are skipped or probed. It helps reduce teaching time. Be careful: we are skipping the TRAINING of some steps that the client can already perform, but the clients must perform ALL the steps of the chain in order, each time.
E.g., if a client can do steps 2 and 3 independently, those will not be trained and the client will have an independent opportunity to complete them in the chain.

3. **Forward Chaining**: a procedure in which a response in a chain is taught one at a time in the same order they naturally occur. The reinforcement is delivered at the end of the step being trained, and previously trained steps are performed independently. It is often used for writing or speaking skills.
E.g., washing hands: the client is given the opportunity to complete step 1 - turn on the tap independently. The remaining steps in the sequence are then taught errorlessly. As the client masters a step, they are then given an independent opportunity to produce that skill. For example, if they are on step 3, it would be expected that they can do steps 1 and 2 independently.

4. **Total Task Chaining**: similar to Forward chaining, but all the steps are trained in every session. The client gets assisted on any step they can't complete independently and gets prompted to proceed to the next step, until they can do the entire chain independently. Prompts are faded using the least-to-most procedure. It is used with learners who have already mastered many steps in the chain but need some practice learning the sequence or they get stuck in some steps.
E.g., For washing hands: the client may be able to do steps 1,2,3 but need help with rinsing the soap off their hands under water, then they may be able to do steps 5 and 6 but require assistance to turn off the tap.

Type	Start teaching	When reinforce?	Use
Backward chaining	Last step	At the end, Natural reinforcer	Self-care skills
Backward chaining with leaps ahead	Last step	At the end, Natural reinforcer	To save teaching time. Probe/skip some steps
Forward chaining	First step	At the end of the step being taught	Writing or speaking skills
Total task chaining	All the steps at once	At the end	With skills that only needs some practice

When a behavior chain is maladaptive, it needs to be interrupted and fixed. Some strategies are:
- Extinction: withhold the SR on a maladaptive link of the chain
- Satiation: provide unlimited access to the SR contingent on the final step of the chain.
- Unchaining: unpairing 2 steps of the chain delivering SR even if the other step doesn't occur.
- Behavior chain interruption strategy: a link in the chain is made unavailable and another behavior is required instead. E.g., instead of eating ice cream after dinner, only fruit is available.
- Substituting the initial SD: substitute the 1st SD of the chain that evokes problem behavior with another SD.
- Extending the chain: adding links in the chain to create time delays for behaviors that need to slow down. E.g., adding 10 min break every 2 hours of work to rest.

G-9 Use Discrete-Trial, Free-Operant, And Naturalistic Teaching Arrangements

Free Operant

In a free-operant teaching arrangement, a discriminative stimulus does not necessarily have to be presented for the response to occur, instead, it can occur at any time (free) and it can occur multiple times.

Reinforcement remains available, and the learner can continue to respond without waiting for a new stimulus to be presented. (no intertrial interval like in DTT)

E.g., a ball may be in the middle of a room and a child picks it up and puts it into a bin. The ball is not necessarily an S(d) for tidying up.

Most research has found that it leads to lower response rates than DTT. It can be used to get baseline data, test for skill generalization, or determine preference.

Discrete-Trial Training (DTT) Lovaas 1960

Instructional method where the student is presented with formal opportunities to perform a skill. Trials are tailored individually to the student, and they are simple, clear, and concise. An SD is provided and a response is systematically taught and reinforced in the presence of the SD. It's a structured procedure where skills are broken down into small units and taught to mastery criteria.

SD --> response --> consequence
Touch nose --> client touches nose --> deliver toy as reinforcement

OR

Touch nose --> client doesn't touch nose --> move to error correction
Repeat SD --> Prompt --> response --> consequence
Touch nose --> Physical prompt --> client touches nose --> lower-level reinforcement (social praise)

We allow the child to practice the skill multiple times in one setting and to contact reinforcement frequently. It is used to teach a wide variety of skills.

It's important to randomly choose the order of the targets within a program and across programs. We also intersperse trials, running mastered targets to promote generalization and ensure maintenance.

This method doesn't resemble the real world so we need to plan for generalization across people and settings.

Different types of DTT:

• Mass trial: involves teaching one exemplar or program at a time with no other trials or programs interspersed and with short pauses between trails. It simply means that you are asking the same target multiple times in a repetitive manner. E.g., Trail 1 "touch dog", Trail 2 "touch dog", Trail 3 "touch dog", ...

• Block trial: intersperse between 1 target in acquisition and 1 target that was previously mastered. E.g., Trail 1 "touch dog"(in acquisition) , Trail 2 "touch dog", Trail 3 "touch cat" (mastered), Trail 3 "touch cat".

• Expanded trial: insert mastered targets between targets in acquisition

• Random rotation: random presentation of mastered targets

Natural Environment Training (AKA: NET, Incidental Teaching, Non intensive teaching) McGee, Daly, Jacobs, 1994

Natural environment training is a method that uses the student's interest and natural motivation to provide structured learning opportunities within naturally occurring activities. It could include discrete and free operant opportunities to learn.

We follow the child's MOs and interests and then we incorporate teaching targets around those. Reinforcers are intermittent, delayed, and unpredictable. NET promotes generalization and maintenance and allows for quick acquisitions due to motivation. It uses stimuli and reinforcers that are already present in the environment so it is considered more socially acceptable and less aversive.

E.g. Lin is completing a puzzle and is almost finished with it, with the exception of the last piece. Lin must request the last piece to earn the reinforcer of completing the puzzle.

A combination of both DTT and NET may be beneficial for the client.

DTT	NET
Highly structured	Loose structure
Contrived	Captured
Instructor led	Student/child led
Discrete learning trials	Free operant
Specific targeted stimuli and scope	Targets selected based on child's motivation
Arbitrary reinforcers	Functionally related reinforcers
Requires special procedures for generalization	Decreased need for programming for generalization

Direct Instruction (DI) Siegfried Engelmann

Direct instruction is an educational method that uses a prepared curriculum in a highly structured with scripted lessons. Main characteristics:

- Teaching in small groups of students according to an individual level. Regrouping based on assessments.
- Face-to-face lessons
- Fast-Paced teaching with frequent assessments
- Scripts followed by teachers
- Signals and Choral Responses of students
- Highly reinforcing teaching techniques for correcting and preventing errors

Precision Teaching (PT) Ogden Lindsley

PT is an individualized instructional method that supports fluency of responding as the main focus for mastery criterion. The charting of students responding on a celeration chart is a component of Precision Teaching. Main characteristics:

- Idea that the "Student is always right."
- Fluency = accuracy + speed = true mastery
- Focus on observable and measurable behaviors
- Uses Celeration Charts
- Used for academic and social behaviors

Personalized System of Instruction (PSI) Keller, 1963

PSI was originally created for college students but then expanded to other levels. The subject matter is broken down into meaningful units, and concepts. Main characteristics:

- Self-paced learning and no punishment for not moving fast enough
- Written materials only, no lectures

- 90% mastery criteria
- Proctors: advanced students help provide feedback to other students and teachers

Programmed Instruction (AKA: Programmed Learning) Skinner

Programmed Instruction is a method used in the classroom to increase the efficiency of learning academic skills.
Main characteristics:

- Self-paced
- Shaping procedure: in order to move to the next step you need to master the current one
- Teaching Machine (computer) provide a question, the student answers usually by filling in the blank, and the machine provides immediate feedback

G-10 Teach Simple And Conditional Discriminations

Discrimination training is a procedure in which a response is reinforced in the presence of a particular stimulus but not in the absence of it. It results in establishing stimulus control. There are different types of discrimination skills: simple discrimination, generalized identity matching, arbitrary visual-visual matching, and auditory-visual matching. The prerequisite skills required for teaching discrimination are:
- Attending
- Scanning
- Tracking
- Selection response

Simple Discrimination

A response is reinforced in the presence of a particular stimulus but not in its absence. It's the most basic type of discrimination skill. E.g., following a simple instruction, responding to your name.
E.g., there is a picture of the letter "A" and a child is asked to find the letter "A".

Conditional Discrimination

A discrimination in which more than one antecedent condition must be present for the response to be reinforced.
Sample stimulus: the target stimulus presented to the learner that will control the target response.
Comparison stimuli: an array of two or more stimuli presented to which the client will respond.
E.g., An array of pictures with a red bird, a blue bird, and a purple bird is presented in front of the child. The instructor then asks to find the red bird. If the client touches any picture other than the red bird, they would not be reinforced; therefore, touching a non-example would result in extinction.

Identity Matching To Sample

Matching the comparison stimuli that look the same as the sample stimulus (physically identical).
It becomes generalized when the client matches stimuli never trained before.
We should start with matching 3D identical objects, then 2D identical pictures.
Note: Matching includes comparison stimuli in which we need to find the identical match to the sample.
Sorting, instead, means putting together items that look the same without comparison stimuli.

Arbitrary Visual-Visual Matching (AKA: Symbolic Matching to Sample, Non-identical matching)

Matching items that do not look exactly the same but still belong together. It includes matching 3D objects to a 2Dpicture of the item (E.g., a picture of a ball with the actual ball) but also nonidentical matching of the same type (E.g., a picture of a soccer ball with a picture of a basketball). Ensure that relevant features are identified.
It is used to identify categories like animals, vehicles, body parts, etc.
It includes Auditory-Visual Matching (AKA receptive language). It means identifying a visual stimulus when presented with an auditory stimulus. E.g., the practitioner says "apple" given an array of stimuli, and the client touches/points to the apple.

Oddity Matching to Sample

The correct comparison is the only 1 not similar to the sample. E.g. in the array I have 3 pictures of dogs and 1 picture of a cat. The sample is a picture of a dog. The correct response is to match it with the cat (the only one different) and get the SR.

G-11 Use Skinner's Analysis To Teach Verbal Behavior

View Task list B-14

Verbal Behavior Theory (VB) is a way to think about human language, including non-spoken communication and thoughts, in functional terms. "Speaker" and "listener" in ABA refer to broad roles not limited to spoken vocal language. Verbal behavior is behavior that is reinforced through the mediation of another person's behavior.

- Speaker: gain access to reinforcement
- Listener: reinforces the speaker

The listener not only plays a critical role as a mediator of reinforcement for the speaker's behavior, but also becomes a discriminative stimulus for the speaker's behavior and functions as an audience.

Theories of Language

- Biological (Chomsky): language is innate to humans
- Cognitive (Bloom, Piaget): language is controlled by internal processing systems that accept, classify, code, encode and store verbal information
- Environmental (Skinner): verbal behavior. Language is a learned behavior, and that is acquired, extended, and maintained by the same types of environmental variables and principles that control non-language behavior

Verbal behavior is the ultimate socially significant behavior and is central to most major aspects of a person's life.

Verbal Operants

Verbal operants are kinds of verbal behavior. They are NOT defined by how they appear (Formal properties of language, E.g., Phonemes, morphemes, lexicon, syntax, grammar, semantics) but rather by the Functional properties of language (function: what need they serve).

The unit of analysis of verbal behavior is the functional relation between a type of responding and the same independent variables that control nonverbal behavior, such as MOs, SD, and consequences.

Types of pure verbal operants:

- Mands: requests. Under functional control of MOs.
- Tacts: labels, names, things, and actions that the speaker has direct contact with through any of the sense modes. It is under the control of a non-verbal stimulus.
- Duplic: Echoic, Mimetic, Copying text. A verbal discriminative stimulus controls it with point-to-point correspondence and formal similarity with the response.
- Codic: Textual, Transcription. Point-to-point correspondence and No formal similarity with the response
- Intraverbals: behavior under the control of someone else's verbal behavior. No formal similarity nor point-to-point correspondence. It's answering questions as well as thinking and talking about events that are not physically present: conversation.
- Listener behavior: behavior under the antecedent control of a mand to comply, and follow simple instructions. Also called Receptive language and Non-verbal compliance. (A) Verbal stimulus- (B) Non-verbal response- (C) Non-specific reinforcer
- Autoclitic: secondary verbal operant, it doesn't occur on its own. It modifies a primary verbal behavior to benefit the listener, add more info, comment, and clarify.

In each one of them, consider the following:

- Point-to-point correspondence: the beginning, middle, and end of the verbal stimulus match the beginning, middle, and end of the verbal response. E.g., Say "boy" with the written word "boy."

- Formal similarity: the controlling antecedent stimulus and the response or response product share the same sense mode and physically resemble each other. E.g., spoken word-spoken word: signed-signed; written-written.

I can have point-to-point correspondence but no formal similarity and vice versa.

Multiple Control

Verbal behavior is controlled by more than one environmental variable. Most of the time, it's what we teach. Rarely we are only teaching pure mands, pure tacts, etc.

Selection-based Verbal Behavior

Verbal behavior in which a speaker selects a stimulus and the listener responds based on the selection. E.g., pointing, selecting, touching items, PECS, electronic device communication system.

The behavior is always the same, the item selected is different.

Topography-based Verbal Behavior

Verbal behavior in which a speaker's response form is different, and the listener responds based on that topography.

- Vocal speech
- Sign language
- Writing words

G-12 Use Equivalence-Based Instruction

Stimulus equivalence is a phenomenon that describes the development of novel stimulus relations following a history of reinforcement for relating stimuli. A derived relation is formed between 2 or more stimuli without direct training due to sameness, differences, comparisons, etc. to trained relations. It's a method to quickly learn new skills by making connections between stimuli that are the same or opposites, stronger or weaker, louder or quieter, etc.

There are three types of stimulus equivalence: reflexivity, symmetry, and transitivity (To remember, R-S-T are in alphabetical order).

1.   Reflexivity (AKA: Generalized Identity Matching):
the client matches A=A (2 identical stimuli), which was never trained.

2.   Symmetry:
the client demonstrates the reversibility of the comparison stimuli. We train that A=B, and the client derives B=A (not trained).

E.g., I train the picture of a car to the text "car", and the client can independently match the text "car" to the image of a car.

E.g., I train that "house" is "casa", and the client derives that "casa" is "house".

3.   Transitivity:
the client derives a stimulus-stimulus relation after being trained on the other two stimulus-stimulus relations. Reflexivity and symmetry must be mastered before transitivity. If taught A=B and B=C, then the client demonstrates A=C.

E.g., I train a picture of the ball and saying "ball", then I train saying "ball" with the written text "ball". The client derives that the picture of the ball is equal to the written text "ball".

Stimulus equivalence is the final step of the sequence after the transitivity phase, where a final symmetry connection is made: if A=B , B=C and A=C then C=A.

An equivalence class is when an individual can consistently make connections without training for many symbolic, arbitrary, or opposite relations. Members of an equivalence class are functionally similar.

G-13 Use The High-Probability Instructional Sequence

High Probability instructional sequence (AKA High-P, Behavioral Momentum)

It's an antecedent intervention where 2/5 easy tasks, called high-p, are presented in quick succession before requesting the target task, the low-p.

High probability tasks are known/mastered tasks, that the client can do fast, without prompts and that are correlated with a history of reinforcers.

The Low probability task is the new target behavior that we want to teach. It requires more effort from the client and the practitioner will deliver a bigger, better reinforcer if completed.

The sequence increases the client's compliance and decreases escape behavior.

It is said that the sequence uses the Behavioral momentum theory that describes the increase in low-p behavior following the series of high-p requests.

E.g., High-p tasks: "give me a high five!", "touch your head", "put your hand on your lap".

E.g., Low-p tasks: "write your name", "read a sentence", "clean up your toys".

E.g., if you are teaching a child to find a picture of a cow (skill in acquisition), you may deliver a high-probability instructional sequence like:

Touch nose --> copy me (waving) --> smile --> touch the cow
(high p) (high p) (high p) (low p)

After each correct response, deliver a quick praise before asking the next task. For the low-p task, deliver the bigger reinforcer if completed correctly and independently.

G-14 Use Reinforcement Procedures To Weaken Behavior (E.g., DRA, FCT, DRO, DRL, NCR)

Differential Reinforcement Procedures
These procedures focus on building functional replacement behaviors for problem behaviors or increasing functionally appropriate behaviors already in a client's repertoire. They involve providing SR for one response class and withholding the SR (Extinction) for another one.
There are many types of differential reinforcement: DRO, DRA, DRI, DRL, DRD, DRH.

Differential Reinforcement Of Other Behavior (DRO, Differential Reinforcement Of Zero Responding)
A procedure in which reinforcement is contingent on the absence/omission of the challenging behavior. SR is given when challenging behavior has not been displayed during a specific time interval or moment.
It is used to decrease the rate of problem behavior and increase the frequency of competing behavior. It's not a constructive procedure like FCT or DRA, we don't teach any new behavior. Procedure:
EXT for the target behavior
SR+ for any other behavior
E.g., if the client has not engaged in hitting behavior for a 5-minute interval, they would receive reinforcement (e.g., iPad for 2 minutes).
Be careful not to accidentally reinforce other non-targeted challenging behavior. E.g., the target is hitting and your client engages in kicking during the DRO interval.

There are different types of DRO:
- DRO Interval: reinforcer is delivered at the end of the interval if the target behavior didn't occur.
- Momentary DRO: reinforcer is delivered at the end of the interval if the target behavior didn't occur at the end of the interval at that moment in time. Challenging behavior can occur during other times within the interval.
- Progressive DRO: same as DRO but reinforcer progressively increases in the amount for successive intervals without target behavior.
Common applications of DRO are: tolerating medical exams or health/hygiene routines.

Differential Reinforcement Of Alternative Behavior (DRA)
Reinforcement is delivered for behavior that is a desirable alternative to the problem behavior but is not necessarily incompatible with it. SR is not provided for the challenging behavior. The alternative behavior is functionally equivalent to the target behavior.
E.g., A child uses biting to attempt to access a preferred item, the 'alternative' behavior may be teaching a functional communication response (e.g., "I want...") which provides an alternative response to get the desired item.
E.g., To escape from a task the child could pull the hair of the therapist or ask for a break (DRA). Both behaviors have the same function but are not incompatible.
Select an alternative behavior that is:
- Lower in effort than the target behavior
- Functionally equivalent
- In the client repertoire
- Not topographically similar
- Reinforced in the client's setting

Start reinforcing every time the alternative behavior occurs, then use a less dense schedule for reinforcement over time.

FCT

Functional communication training is a subtype of DRA that specifically involves verbal behavior. It teaches manding as an alternative to problem behavior.

2 types of manding:
- Specific mand. E.g., drink water, sandwich, more toys, etc.
- Omnibus mand (generalized). E.g., food, more, want, etc.

Differential Reinforcement Of Incompatible Behavior (DRI)

This intervention is a variation of DRA and involves reinforcing a behavior that cannot physically occur during the same time as the problem behavior. The challenging behavior and the alternative behavior are mutually exclusive. E.g., if a student hits other children while transitioning through the hallways at school, an 'incompatible' behavior would be keeping their hands in their pocket while walking. In this example, you can't both be hitting and have both hands in your pocket, as it's not physically possible.

Differential Negative Reinforcement Of Incompatible/Alternative behavior (DNRA/DNRA)

The alternative/incompatible behavior is reinforced with an escape from the demand. This procedure is specifically used when the challenging behavior is maintained by escape.
E.g., the child asks for a break instead of running away to escape the demand from the teacher.

Differential Reinforcement Of Low Rates (DRL)

Reinforcement is provided only if the rate of responses is equal to or lower than a predetermined criterion. It is used to decrease the rate of responding but not to get to zero rates. This is typically used for socially acceptable behaviors but may occur too often. Do not use it for dangerous behavior.

E.g., if a student speaks out of turn in class too frequently, you want to lower this behavior. Still, it may never necessarily be completely at zero, which might be realistic/tolerable in a social setting. This intervention delivers reinforcement if a behavior occurs below a predetermined level/criterion. So, if that student spoke out of turn 10 or fewer times during their math lesson, he would gain access to a reinforcer.

The criterion is placed below the average baseline rate. 3 types of DRL:
- Interval DRL
- Full session DRL
- Spaced responding DRL: based on IRT. The reinforcement is delivered after a minimum amount of time elapsed since the last response. E.g., a snack is delivered if at least 1h has elapsed since the previous snack.

Differential Reinforcement Of Diminishing Rates Of Behavior (DRD)

This intervention involves reinforcing a progressively lower criterion of the target behavior. This is used for problem behaviors that are displayed too frequently but that we don't want to eliminate entirely. E.g., I earn an SR after eating 4 or fewer snacks during the day. The criteria would continue to go lower (e.g., starting at 4 and lowering to 3, then 2, until 1 per day). We don't want to remove access to a snack during the day altogether.

Non-Contingent Reinforcement NCR

Noncontingent reinforcement means delivering the reinforcement independently of the target behavior but on a time-based schedule. We are not teaching any new or alternative behavior, but we are altering the MOs.

E.g., if an NCR procedure were using social praise as reinforcement on a FI 5 minutes schedule, every 5 minutes, regardless of what the client is doing, they would receive social praise from staff. The purpose of the process is to grant access/satiate the individual from the reinforcer maintaining the problem behavior. In this example, if the child is always attention-seeking and engaging in problem behavior to get negative attention, the NCR procedure would give this client an influx of attention with the intent to teach the client that they don't have to engage in problem behavior to gain access to attention.

Differential Reinforcement Of High Rates (DRH)

This procedure is used to increase behavior that your client displays too infrequently. The reinforcer is provided for emitting behaviors that are at or above a pre-established criterion. There are 3 types:

- Interval DRH
- Full session DRH
- Spaced responding DRH

E.g., I get a reinforcer when I work out at the gym 2 or more times per week.

G-15 Use Extinction (AKA: Operant Extinction)
view Task List B-9

Extinction is a procedure that provides zero possibility of reinforcement. It occurs when reinforcement of a previously reinforced behavior is discontinued or withheld. As result, the frequency of that behavior decreases in the future.

Unwanted Effects Of Extinction
1)   Extinction burst
2)   Increase in the magnitude of the response
3)   Extinction-induced response variation
4)   Extinction-induced aggression
5)   Emotional responses
6)   Spontaneous recovery
7)   Resurgence
8)   Behavioral contrast

G-16 Use Positive And Negative Punishment (E.g., Time-Out, Response Cost, Overcorrection)

view Task List B-6

Punishment

Environmental change that follows a response closely in time, is contingent on that response and decreases the probability of similar responses under similar circumstances.

Positive Punishment

Adding an aversive stimulus to the environment as the consequence of undesirable behavior, decreases the behavior. Positive punishers' procedures are:

1)   Verbal Reprimands
2)   Contingent exercise
3)   Response blocking
4)   Response interruption and redirection (RIRD
5)   Physical restraint
6)   Overcorrection: Restitutional or Positive Practice
7)   Contingent aversive stimuli with problem behavior

Negative Punishment

Removing an appetitive stimulus from the environment as the consequence of undesirable behavior, decreases the behavior.

Negative punishers' procedures are:

1)   Response cost
2)   Exclusionary Time out
3)   Non-exclusionary Time out

G-17 Use Token Economies (AKA: Token System)

Token Economy

It is a behavior change program in which symbols, tokens, are earned based on specified behaviors followed by token exchange for rewards.

Tokens are generalized condition reinforcers because they have been paired with a variety of reinforcers.

Procedure:
- Identify behavior
- Select tokens: consider cost, durability, client preferences, and ease of delivery. E.g., points, stickers, stars, etc.
- Select items for exchange: tangibles, activities, breaks, etc
- Establish earning/exchange ratio: number of responses required for token delivery and number of tokens required to redeem a backup reinforcer
- Develop procedure: when to deliver tokens, when to exchange reinforcers and how
- Test and train staff

Ensure the client possesses the prerequisite skills for the behaviors targeted for a token economy to be successful. Tokens should be obtainable and not overly difficult to earn, otherwise, the student would not be able to contact reinforcement, and this would reduce the effectiveness of the procedure.

Remember that the procedure should be faded out over time.

Level System

It's a type of token economy in which participants move up a hierarchy of tiers contingent on meeting specific performance criteria with respect to the target behaviors.

The client moves up/down the levels based on his behavior, and each level is associated with different amounts of privilege and reinforcers.

Usually used with higher functioning individuals but be careful because it could become punitive.

G-18 Use Group Contingencies

In a group contingency, a common consequence is contingent on the behavior of one member of the group, the behavior of part of the group, or the behavior of everyone in the group.

This procedure can save time and reduce workload by applying consequences to more than one client. It can benefit from peer influence and facilitate positive interactions but could also result in negative peer pressure.

Group contingencies are the following:

1. Independent Group Contingency

Each individual earns their own consequence, but it's available for everyone. It's fair but not individualized, and there's minimal peer support.

E.g., every student who can complete all 15 math questions before recess starts will get to stay outside for an additional time. Anyone who does not complete the 15 math questions before recess does not get the extra time outside.

2. Dependent Group Contingency (AKA: Hero procedure)

Rewarding the entire group based on the work of one individual. Peers can encourage the individual or put too much pressure on him.

E.g., the soccer team has a final shot at winning the game. The player selected must score the goal for the team to win.

3. Interdependent Group Contingency

The entire group needs to meet the goal to receive reinforcement. It's an "all or none" arrangement where all students earn the rewards or none of them. Variations can include earning rewards contingent on a group average. It encourages group cohesiveness. A limitation is that the whole group fails if one person stops working.

E.g., every member of the group needs to complete their math worksheet with 15 questions for the entire class to get the extra recess time.

4. Indiscriminable Group Contingency

The individual does not know whether or not the next response will be reinforced. No one can predict when the reward will be delivered. Everyone works harder to meet the criterion and promotes generalization and maintenance.

G-19 Use Contingency Contracting (AKA: Behavioral Contract)

A contingency contract is a document that specifies a contingent relationship between the completion of a target behavior and access to a specified reward. It stipulates how 2 or more people will behave toward each other. It can also be a self-contract that a person makes with oneself and it promotes self-management skills.

It's a permanent product that uses rule-governed behavior. It must be written but symbols can be used between one adult and a small child.

Uses:
- Increase behaviors already in the repertoire
- Decrease inappropriate behaviors
- Improve academic responding

Elements:
- Beginning and end date
- Specify performance (target behavior, who, what, when, how well)
- Specify the consequence (the reward, kind, amount, when)
- Schedule review progress
- Data collection for task completion and reward delivery
- Signatures

Occasionally it may be necessary to incorporate a response cost contingencies, the removal of rewards, if the agreed task was not completed.

Shhh...

G-20 Use Self-Management Strategies

Self-management involves a person applying behavior change tactics to their own behavior to produce the desired change. It is used to break bad habits, form good ones, achieve personal goals, and improve life.
Self-control entails responding to a delayed but larger or higher quality reinforcer instead of acting to obtain an immediate, less valuable, reinforcer. A person can use self-management to achieve self-control.

Procedure:
•   Define behavior and specify the goal
•   Self-measurement, data collection: it requires the person to observe and record their own behavior occurrence and nonoccurrence.
•   Assist/contrive competing contingencies for target behavior change: identify precursors, use prompts (e.g., reminders), use MOs, remove necessary items, perform alternative or incompatible behaviors, perform initial steps of a chain (e.g., put the vacuum in the middle of the room as a prompt for later).
•   Make it public, and talk about it with others.
•   Use an accountability partner and make regular contact daily/weekly
•   Support and evaluate. Self-evaluation compares her performance with a predetermined goal or standard, it can be aided by self-graphing collected data.
The advantage is that it "feels good," but also it's challenging to implement.
It requires rule governance, and contingencies must be consistently implemented to be effective.

Some tactics used in self-management:
•   Antecedent-based self-management strategies include manipulating MOs, providing response prompts like reminders for desired behaviors, initiating a behavior chain, environmental planning, and limiting challenging behavior to restricted stimulus conditions.
•   Self-monitoring (AKA: Self-Recording, Self-Observation) involves a person observing their own behavior and recording their own target behavior's occurrence or non-occurrence. E.g., someone trying to follow a diet may be using an application on their phone to track their food intake and calories.
•   Self-evaluation involves a person comparing their own performance to a predetermined goal or standard.
•   Self-instruction involves a person using their own self-generated verbal responses (covert or overt) to provide a response prompt for the desired behavior. In essence, a person tells themself what to do.
•   Habit reversal involves "a multi-component treatment package" that consists of a person becoming aware of their habit, interrupting their habit, using a competing behavior, and rewarding themself while also accessing social support systems.
•   Systematic desensitization involves a self-directed substitution of one behavior for an unwanted behavior (usually replacing fear and anxiety with muscle relaxation). The client learns to relax in imaginary situations and then gradually in real-life situations.
•   Massed Practice (AKA: Negative Practice) is forcing oneself to perform an undesired behavior repeatedly. This will sometimes decrease the future occurrences of the behavior but it's unhealthy and not evidence based.

G-21 Use Procedures To Promote Stimulus And Response Generalization
view Task List B-11

When the behavior occurs outside of training conditions or when relevant and untaught behavior variance appears, we can say that generalization occurred.
There are 2 types of generalization:

1) Stimulus Generalization
Spread of effects of training to stimuli not present during training. The behavior is the same but occurs in different settings, with different people, or with different items.

2) Response Generalization
Spread of effects of reinforcement to other similar reinforced responses. Different behaviors are occurring in the same stimulus condition.

G-22 Use procedures To Promote Maintenance (AKA: Response Maintenance)

Maintenance is the continued effect of an intervention in the absence of the intervention.

How to program for maintenance:
- Use intermittent schedules for reinforcement (VI-VR)
- Increase delay in delivery of the reinforcement
- The skill accesses reinforcement in the natural environment.

E.g., teaching an individual to cook a meal is likely to be maintained because food is a primary reinforcer. Teaching a client how to do calculus is less likely to be maintained if the skill is not being used frequently and/or isn't accessing reinforcement.
- Skill is taught to fluency: consider using a mastery criteria higher than 80%.
- Repetition: the more practice an individual has with doing a skill, the more likely it is to maintain.

The lasting change of the behavior is the ultimate goal of every program so, if the behavior is not maintained over time we failed the treatment.
E.g., check if a client can still tie their shoes a week after it has been mastered.

Coffee and Notes:

....

....

....

....

....

....

....

....

....

....

....

....

....

....

....

....

....

....

....

H.   **Behavior-Change Procedures**

H-1:   State intervention goals in observable and measurable terms.

H-2:   Identify potential interventions based on assessment results and the best available scientific evidence.

H-3:   Recommend intervention goals and strategies based on such factors as client preferences, supporting environments, risks, constraints, and social validity.

H-4:   When a target behavior is to be decreased, select an acceptable alternative behavior to be established or increased.

H-5:   Plan for possible unwanted effects when using reinforcement, extinction, and punishment procedures.

H-6:   Monitor client progress and treatment integrity.

H-7:   Make data-based decisions about the effectiveness of the intervention and the need for treatment revision.

H-8:   Make data-based decisions about the need for ongoing services.

H-9:   Collaborate with others who support and/or provide services to clients.

H-1 State Intervention Goals In Observable And Measurable Terms

view Task List C-1

Goal Objectives

You must have goal objectives to know when to terminate treatment or to assess the effectiveness of the intervention. Goal objectives must be written and approved by your clients before implementation.

Objectives consist of:

- Target behavior: operationally defined in a clear, objective, and concise manner.
- Specific conditions where the behavior is expected to occur
- Mastery criteria
- Other dimensions (magnitude, latency, duration, etc.)

Acquisition targets: skill deficits taught to improve their learners' quality of life
E.g., dressing, feeding, playing skills, etc.

Reduction targets: problem behaviors that interfere with the consumer's quality of life. E.g., SIB, physical aggression, etc.

H-2 Identify Potential Interventions Based On Assessment Results And The Best Available Scientific Evidence

After you complete an FBA, you can use all available information to design your intervention and treatment plan based on your FBA results.

Take into consideration:

- Client preference: what the client wants and doesn't want
- Assessment results: what did the FBA say? What is the function of the behavior? Look at indirect, direct, and functional analysis data.
- Scientific evidence: You are obligated to remain up to date on research and choose the most effective procedure. Research is ongoing, stay informed and maintain knowledge of current scientific info. You can also consult with other experts and professionals.
- Other factors: preference assessments, medical assessments, prior intervention history

An FBA indicates if your client's behavior needs to be:

- Established: teach a new skill
- Maintained
- Increased/decreased
- Eliminated
- Left alone

Discrepancy Analysis

It is used to compare a client's behavior to same-age, typically developing peers to determine if a challenging behavior is at problematic levels or appropriate for that age. It defines behavioral standards for acceptability.

H-3 Recommend Intervention Goals And Strategies Based On Such Factors As Client Preferences, Supporting Environments, Risks, Constraints, And Social Validity

As previously mentioned, after assessing the function of the behavior, you need to decide what treatment is best to use.

Several considerations are needed for choosing the best intervention for the client.

Environment and Resources:

- Where does the treatment take place? Is the environment set up to handle the intervention?
- Is everyone in the environment committed to carry out the intervention to meet the goals?
- Identify available resources
- Collaborate with key people
- Staff-to-client ratio: E.g., lots of clients and few staff members
- Availability of reinforcers
- Ability to provide preferred stimuli, E.g., snacks acceptable at school?
- Identify disruptions to the environment and try to solve them. Document all the attempts and solutions.
- Outside influences, E.g., attention from other people (at the mall) when extinction treatment is in place.

Treatment Fidelity:

- Who is implementing the treatment?
- Is staff training needed? Is oversight necessary?
- Are errors impacting the treatment effectiveness?

2 types: Omission errors (not reinforcing the alternative behavior when needed) and Commission errors (reinforcing the problem behavior when it occurs).

Client Preference:

- Consider the preferences of the client but also of the caregivers. The client should be involved in the treatment planning to the fullest extent possible. This is part of maintaining the client's dignity.
- Goals can be negotiated.
- Consider the family values, culture, and concerns
- Assess and value the current client's strengths.

Safety:

- Do no harm

Social Validity:

- Whether the goals of the planned intervention are acceptable
- Whether the procedures are acceptable and aligned with best treatment practices
- Whether the obtained results show meaningful, significant, and sustainable change

Ethically, the behavior analyst must carefully consider whether a particular goal should be accomplished and whether the achievement of the goal would be sustainable in the natural environment.

Cost-Benefit Analysis:

- Compare the cost of a treatment or intervention and the projected benefits. The benefit to the individual should be significant enough to justify the short and long-term cost of providing the service.

Risk-Benefit Analysis:
- Assess the general risk factors for behavioral treatment
- Assess the risk factors for each behavioral procedure
- Assess the benefits of behavioral treatment
- Reconcile the risk and benefits with the key parties involved
- Minimize and/or prepare for the risks as much as possible

H-4 When A Target Behavior Is To Be Decreased, Select An Acceptable Alternative Behavior To Be Established Or Increased

All behavior serves a function. If you eliminate a behavior, you remove a functional action from the learner's repertoire. It is an obligation to replace that behavior with another functionally equivalent one.

Fair Pair Rule: whenever behavior is decreased, another behavior must increase in its place.

Functional Equivalent: the behavior must serve the same function.
E.g., if you remove aggression to gain attention from mom, you need to replace it with an equivalent functional behavior such as communication. (FCT)

H-5 Plan For Possible Unwanted Effects When Using Reinforcement, Extinction, And Punishment Procedures

Unwanted Effects Of Reinforcement (view Task List see B-4)

Unwanted Effects Of Extinction (view Task List see B-9)

Unwanted Effects Of Punishment (view Task List see B-6)

H-6 Monitor Client Progress And Treatment Integrity

Client progress must be monitored systematically to assess the efficacy of the treatment and make changes as dictated by the data. Assessment is ongoing and never ends.

Treatment Integrity
It is the extent to which the procedure is implemented correctly as planned. To assess it, you can verify if the written intervention matches the actual implementation of the treatment.

Procedural Fidelity
It is the extent to which the procedure in ALL conditions (baseline and treatment) is being implemented correctly.

Threats to Treatment Integrity
•	Treatment Drift: The gradual (and often accidental) change in how the treatment is implemented over time. The application of the IV is different in later phases compared to the original intended application.
E.g., On day1 the reinforcement schedule was FR2. The supervisees, after a month, are now implementing a VR3 reinforcement schedule. Treatment has started to drift.
•	Experimenter bias
•	Acceptability of the IVs by the implementer
•	The implementer prefers some aspects of the IV but not others

To ensure high levels of treatment integrity provide training and support to the staff, specify the procedures, and use simpler and positive IVs that are more acceptable.

H-7 Make Data-Based Decisions About The Effectiveness Of The Intervention And The Need For Treatment Revision

An effective treatment produces the intended, desired result.
The practitioner needs to always analyze the data and then decide:
•	Continue with the intervention: no changes are necessary because the treatment is effective and you see progress in the right direction
•	Modify some aspects of the intervention that is in place
•	Discontinue the intervention: the data shows there is no progress and the treatment is ineffective. Stop the treatment and start designing and implementing another one is the best decision.

H-8 Make Data-Based Decisions About The Need For Ongoing Services

The decision to continue services should be data-driven and needs-based.

Data-driven: does the data indicate that interventions are still needed to increase or decrease target behaviors? Everything we do should be based on data!

Needs-based: Once goals are met and no other goals are identified, it is time to transition services. Always consider:
- Are services benefiting the client?
- Are we targeting socially significant behaviors?
- Have we failed to achieve any goals?
- Have we failed to make progress?

Do not abandon clients! We always plan for transitions.

H-9 Collaborate With Others Who Support And/Or Provide Services To Clients

Collaboration is working with others to achieve the same goals for our clients. We want to produce positive and beneficial outcomes.

Parent Training
Collaborate with caregivers to optimize treatment for their circumstances, context, and resources. Parents are part of the team. We must ensure they are properly trained and involved in the planning of the interventions.

Multidisciplinary Team
A group of individuals that provide a specific service to the client.
E.g., the client receives ABA, OT, speech therapy, and attends school. This is his team.
Often we work as part of an interdisciplinary team, sometimes converging upon the same behavior targets. Different team members may prescribe different interventions for a client. Ideally, all team members are aware of every intervention and how interventions may potentially interact. Collaboration benefits include:
- Frequent updates of progress between professionals
- Joint problem solving
- Collective progress evaluation

In general:
- Share information: after signing confidentiality agreements, you should share data and progress info with the rest of the team.
- Obtain information: seek info from other practitioners when necessary
- Attend meetings (E.g., IEP meeting)
- Accept feedback and input from others. Offer to take data for other interventions suggested and provide results.
- Prioritize the best interest of the client
- Find, understand, and provide the available evidence: share your research with your colleagues
- Discuss behavioral interventions using accessible language and explain the rationale behind the function-based model
- Communicate behavioral concepts, avoid jargon and minimize behavior-specific data display.
- Be aware of other's ethical boundaries but maintain your own
- If the client chooses to participate in an intervention that is disruptive to their behavioral treatment, you must withdraw your treatment

We are mostly working with:

Speech-Language Pathologist (SLP)
There is a strong relationship between problem behavior and communication: high communication problem evokes high rates of problem behavior, especially SIB.
SLP focus on communication, social skills development, speech, language, oral mechanisms, swallowing disorders, and pre-linguistic skills.
One clear area of intersection is the use of FCT (Functional Communication Training) which means reinforcing an alternative communicative response by providing assess to the consequence determined by the FA.

Occupational Therapist (OT)

OT helps people work on cognitive, physical, social, and motor skills. The goal is to become more independent and participate in a wide range of everyday activities. They place emphasis on assessing sensory-motor, emotional regulation, independent living skills, motor development, and self-regulation strategies.

Sensory processing disorder can be a cause of problem behavior, this means the child can be over-responsive or unresponsive to a particular sensory input.

OT and behavior analysts can work together to understand and reduce the problem behavior.

Coffee and Notes:

I.   Personnel Supervision And Management

I-1:   State the reasons for using behavior-analytic supervision and the potential risks of ineffective supervision (e.g., poor client outcomes, poor supervisee performance

I-2:   Establish clear performance expectations for the supervisor and supervisee.

I-3:   Select supervision goals based on an assessment of the supervisee's skills.

I-4:   Train personnel to competently perform assessment and intervention procedures.

I-5:   Use performance monitoring, feedback, and reinforcement systems.

I-6:   Use a functional assessment approach (e.g., performance diagnostics) to identify variables affecting personnel performance.

I-7:   Use function-based strategies to improve personnel performance.

I-8:   Evaluate the effects of supervision (e.g., on client outcomes, on supervisee repertoires).

I-1 State The Reasons For Using Behavior-Analytic Supervision And The Potential Risks Of Ineffective Supervision (E.g., Poor Client Outcomes, Poor Supervisee Performance

BA Supervision

Behavior analytic supervision ensures treatment is being provided properly, supervisees are well trained, and provide the best chance of optimal outcomes. The purpose is to ensure that behavior-analytic services are delivered effectively and ethically.

A competency-based supervision experience that harnesses behavior analytic principles will provide a rich experience for supervisees. Assessment of skills, goal setting, and utilizing effective feedback, among many other strategies backed by the literature, are all critical in developing early-career professionals.

• Use a competency-based curriculum (scope and content): Will you provide training on the entire task list? Is it all within your area of competence? How will skills/items be grouped? What are the mastery criteria for each item?
• Assess performance (initial and ongoing)
• Teach content (Behavioral Skills Training)
• Monitor performance: Data-based decision making

Our scope of practice as behavior analysts is quite broad, but our scope of competence is much narrower. This applies to supervision as well! We should only provide supervision within the context of our area of competence. This is where supervision under multiple supervisors can be highly beneficial!

E.g., If my scope of competence is limited to OBM, I am not engaged in ethical supervision if my supervisee is working with clients who engage in self-injurious behavior. I may be able to supervise the use of DRA in an OBM setting, but not with the client who engages in self-injury.

The role of the BCBA is to ensure that staff is adequately trained and can deliver interventions with a degree of fidelity that will lead to effective outcomes.

When staff is not adequately supported, this results in the following:

• Client outcomes suffer
• Staff feels lonely, confused, not motivated, and incompetent.
• A hostile work environment with possible high turnover rates and staff absenteeism.
• Possible ethical violations
• Negative implications for your organization financially.

I-2 Establish Clear Performance Expectations For The Supervisor And Supervisee

Supervisees should have clear goals and expectations from the outset of supervision.

Supervisors should also have goals in terms of how they will provide supervision.

Everything should be data-based: Supervisors and supervisees should have a data recording system in place to ensure targets are being met and goals are being mastered. If goals and expectations are not set, supervision is not appropriate.

As mentioned in our Ethic Code, all supervisors and supervisees must sign the supervision contract before starting supervision. We must retain all the supervision documentation for at least 7 years.

The primary purpose of behavior analytic supervision is to ensure the trainee's behavior changes due to the training provided.

What should be included in performance expectations:

1.   A description of specific job tasks (e.g., taking data, preparing client materials, writing session notes, etc.).

2.   A description of who will be responsible for each task (e.g., supervisor or supervisee).

3.   A set timeline for specific job duties to be completed (e.g., daily, weekly, monthly, etc.).

4.   A measurement system to determine if job duties are completed on time (e.g., job checklist with each task).

5.   A schedule of meetings/check-ins to determine the progress of job duties (e.g., weekly, monthly etc.).

6.   A method of feedback and documentation regarding the job duties (e.g., performance appraisal, meeting notes, etc.). Always appreciate and consider input from RBTs, colleagues, trainees, and other professionals.

I-3 Select Supervision Goals Based On An Assessment Of The Supervisee's Skills

The supervisee should be made aware that you will assess their skills before the assessment. There are various ways to assess a supervisee's competency, with some being more empirical than others. A self-assessment is a quick but possibly inaccurate way of determining areas of strength/growth. Activities like roleplay or observing duties with performance checklists are more time-intensive but often yield a more accurate understanding of a supervisee's competency. Like any goal/target we track, the skills being assessed should be operationally defined in observable and measurable terms. Data should be collected on each of these skills to determine what level of skill the supervisee has with implementing each target.

Goals based on current ability are foundational in creating a productive, meaningful supervision experience. Our goal as supervisors should be to set our supervisees up to contact reinforcement as much as possible throughout supervision. Setting reasonable goals based on assessment helps!

Use SMART goals:

S=Specific: set goals operationally defined with real numbers with real deadlines

M=Measurable: select goals that are measurable and observable to track data

A= Attainable: work towards goals that are challenging but possible. You can always increase the difficulty or complexity gradually.

R= Realistic: set goals that are achievable. You know what you and your team are capable of.

T= Timely: goals should have a deadline to be achieved or evaluated

I-4 Train Personnel To Competently Perform Assessment And Intervention Procedures

Prior to participating in assessment or intervention procedures, supervisees should be trained to competence utilizing evidence-based training procedures (hint, BST!). Competency-based training ensures service providers are capable of delivering proper service. RBTs are essential in the service delivery system and play a tremendous role in the outcome of clients. It is our job to train them properly and ensure they implement the treatments correctly. BST involves:

- Describe the skill: what skill are you training? What is the goal?
- Written plan: what do you hope to accomplish?
- Model the skill: perform the skill for your supervisee. (show)
- Role play: act out the skill
- Observe the supervisee implementing the skill in a real scenario
- Provide feedback: constructive feedback regarding the skill, reinforce performance
- Repeat until mastery

Our protocols are only as good as our staff is able to implement them. Utilizing evidence-based training procedures is crucial. Our clients deserve effective treatment, and our supervisees deserve proper support from us. When the client fails to progress, our first question should be, was the intervention done with fidelity?

I-5 Use Performance Monitoring, Feedback, And Reinforcement Systems

Performance monitoring

Performance monitoring involves monitoring a supervisee's performance. Now that they have specific goals in place, the supervisor must follow up on these goals to ensure that the supervisee is on the right path to achieving them.

It includes formal and informal observations and assessments that can evaluate the maintenance and generalization of the skills. Performance monitoring should happen routinely at least once a month, if not more. It uses the same data collection that we use with the clients.

1.   Direct

Observation of implementation in the field or during role-play (be aware of reactivity.)

- Knowledge of the treatment plan.
- Treatment integrity.
- Understand the ABA concepts.
- Interaction with stakeholders.

2.   Indirect

Supervisees report their experiences or fill out rating scales for themselves.

Feedback

It should be directed, constructive, and based on the implementation of services. The best time to provide feedback is immediately after the observation so that all of the skills demonstrated during the observation are still recent. Feedback should also be documented.

- Identify what was done correctly and incorrectly and be specific.
- Identify what can be improved.
- Identify how to improve.
- Allow the supervisee to ask questions.
- Try to keep it positive.

3 main types of feedback:

- Adequacy (what was done well). E.g., Jimmy, amazing job creating that task analysis!
- Diagnostic (what was done incorrectly). E.g., Jimmy, your praise was general instead of specific.
- Corrective (what to fix and how). E.g., Jimmy, next time name what the client is doing when praising them.

Reinforcement system

Always reinforce correct supervisee behavior with praise and conditioned/unconditioned reinforcers.

Supervisee monitoring is very similar to client monitoring. Use reinforcement to strengthen behaviors you want to see more often in the future. It is highly individual!

E.g., Performance-based pay or bonuses, contingent praise, attention, access to new or more desirable status, responsibilities, extended lunch breaks, etc.

It is important to remember that reinforcement must occur even when everything is going well to maintain these positive behaviors.

I-6 Use A Functional Assessment Approach (E.g., Performance Diagnostics) To Identify Variables Affecting Personnel Performance

Establish goals the same way we would set goals for clients. Supervisors should use a functional approach when performance issues arise to understand the problem (why is this happening?).

Just as we would determine the function of a client's behavior, it is important to consider the function of a supervisee's behavior. For example, a supervisee who tends to call in sick on days they are scheduled to meet for feedback may be a pattern of escape-maintained behavior. To help alleviate this situation, it is important to understand how your supervisee would like to receive feedback and how they would like to demonstrate their skills and abilities. Some supervisees may prefer written feedback with brief social interactions, which is okay if that works best for them.

Use different functional assessments to obtain information regarding the function of your supervisee's behavior:

•   Indirect: an interview with the supervisee to identify areas the supervisee needs more support/training. Also, questionnaires or surveys can be useful tools.

•   Direct: directly observe your supervisee with clients, parents, and other staff. Look to see how their environment could better support the supervisee.

PDC-HS (Performance Diagnostic Checklist- Human Services) is a great tool for this.

Once you can determine the function of their behavior, this will allow you to start the problem-solving process of determining strategies to help them be successful.

I-7 Use Function-Based Strategies To Improve Personnel Performance

Function-based strategies are effective because they can assist in identifying relevant environmental conditions that can be modified to help promote the desired performance.

Once supervisors have identified why a supervisee's performance needs improvement, the supervisor plans an intervention to address those factors.

So you've identified the function of the problem, now what?

- Insufficient training? Train them using Behavioral Skills Training
- Task clarification needed? Provide checklists, prompts
- Insufficient resources, materials, or processes? Redesign materials/processes
- Insufficient effort or environmental consequences? Be more present as a supervisor, provide more frequent feedback, and reduce response effort.

Strategies For Escape Maintained Behavior

Alternative methods of supervision can be offered as a potential solution so that the individual doesn't have to use sick time to avoid situations. A reinforcement approach can also be used to have the supervisee earn additional paid time off, which may give them a more appropriate way of accessing escape.

Strategies For Attention-Maintained Behavior

Similar to escape behavior, offering the supervisee a variety of different options to demonstrate their skills without direct observation may be a functional way for the supervisee to demonstrate the skills without the intimidation of being supervised. Systematic desensitization may also be used to offer the supervisee a way to demonstrate their strongest skill live and then continue to increase the length of observation time systematically.

Strategies For Tangible Maintained Behavior

If possible, set up contingencies where the individual needs to complete set tasks to gain access to tangible goods. Depending on the tangible, this could be made contingent on performance goals and job requirements. If they are interested in making more money, you could expand services to include evening and weekend groups to create additional opportunities to earn income for the supervisee.

Strategies For Sensory Maintained Behavior

This would likely focus more on negative reinforcement. For example, a company-wide policy may request a scent-free work environment if someone is sensitive to smells. Environmental modifications could make workspaces quieter, brighter, and more open for other sensory needs.

I-8 Evaluate The Effects Of Supervision (E.g., On Client Outcomes, On Supervisee Repertoires)

Supervisors and supervisees should use data to evaluate how the supervisee is progressing and compare client acquisition data when the supervisee is working with those clients.

Supervisee

The supervisor can create checklists, and feedback forms for the supervisee's to complete regarding their experience with supervision. These forms must remain anonymous to ensure that feedback is reflective of their true feelings.

The supervisor could also have the supervisees do some self-reflection on their own skills and complete some self-monitoring checklists to determine if the supervisee feels they are making progress.

If the supervision is effective, the supervisee should be making progress in the following skills:

- Professional skills: Time management skills, Interpersonal skills
- Fluency of knowledge
- Time from introduction of skills to generalization/maintenance

Clients

The supervisor can create checklists and feedback forms for clients/families to complete regarding their experience with the behavior analytic service.

- Are interventions appropriately matched to clients?
- Is the client making progress? At what rate are they making progress?
- Are skills generalizing and maintaining?
- Is the therapeutic relationship strong?

Supervisor

The supervisor could do some self-reflection on their own skills and complete self-monitoring checklists to determine if they feel they are delivering effective supervision.

Coffee and Notes:

Appendix

Now get your bonus by scanning the QR code.

AudioBook

Are you looking for the entire 6 hours audiobook?
Scan the two QR codes here and start listening.

Don't forget your Gift

Our special bonus will enrich your reading experience. this book has many suplementary materials to enhance your comprehension, knowledge, skills, and information.

Made in the USA
Middletown, DE
20 July 2023

35487124R00104